Human Remains

INTERPRETING·THE·PAST

HUMAN REMAINS

Andrew Chamberlain

Published for the Trustees of the British Museum
by British Museum Press

Acknowledgements

While writing this book I received help and encouragement from Nina Shandloff and Joanna Champness at British Museum Press, and special thanks are due to Beth Rega, Sheridan Bowman and Don Brothwell, whose helpful suggestions improved the book in many ways. I am also grateful to the following for supplying me with illustrative material:

cover: Trustees of the British Museum; **figure 1:** Susan Goodfield; **6:** Wiley-Liss and Robert Hoppa; **14:** Dr E. Tapp; **17:** Dr Charlotte Roberts; **24:** National Museums and Galleries on Merseyside; **25:** Trustees of the British Museum; **26:** Greenland Museum; **27:** Sygma; **28:** James Hancock; **29:** John Hinchcliffe and the editor of *The Archaeological Journal*; **31:** Claire Adamson; **32:** Dr Harold Mytum, University of York; **33:** Bristol City Museum and Art Gallery; **35:** Dr Mike Parker Pearson; **37:** Mariana Yampolsky.

Designed by Andrew Shoolbred

Set in Compugraphic Palacio and printed in
Great Britain by The Bath Press, Avon

ISBN 0-7141-2092-5

A catalogue record for this book is available from
the British Library

Cover illustration: An ancient human body found in a bog at Lindow Moss, Cheshire, in 1984. The body is of an adult male who has been ritually killed before being deposited in a pool in the bog.

Contents

Preface

Humans have buried their dead for the last fifty thousand years. Their monuments and grave goods have been the study of antiquarians for several centuries but recent advances in medicine and science now allow the human remains themselves to be investigated, revealing details about the people and the communities to which they belonged.

Modern methods of forensic anthropology can reveal the age of the skeleton as well as its sex, stature and some aspects of its ancestry. Bones and teeth retrieved by archaeologists often show evidence of injury and infection and even sometimes the signs of a violent end. Physical stresses and degenerative changes are detected on the bones, showing the difficulties suffered by people for whom medical care was rudimentary. Fascinating insights into prehistoric social life are given by skeletons of people who, despite being too handicapped to have played an active role in subsistence, nevertheless survived to a good age.

An exciting new development in the study of human skeletons stems from the techniques of molecular biology which now allow DNA and proteins to be extracted from archaeological bone. These biomolecules can be matched between individuals and populations, providing the basis for the study of kinship relations and the migrations of populations as well as increasing scientists' understanding of human genetic diversity.

For the archaeologist the human skeleton is sometimes an awkward 'find' that may seem time-consuming and complicated to record and excavate. Unlike that of most other finds, the legal status of buried skeletons can be uncertain, and the excavator also needs to be aware of the sensibilities of local communities. The opportunity to research the skeletal biology of past populations is nevertheless a valuable one, even when the remains are ultimately destined for reburial.

— 1 —

Identifying Human Bones

Human or non-human?

One of the first questions to be asked of any bone is whether it is, in fact, human at all. Overall size, shape and texture are the main criteria by which bones can be judged to belong to humans or to another animal species, but there are also differences at the microscopic level. When a thin section of bone is viewed under a microscope, concentric structures known as osteons are seen (fig. **1**). The osteons in human bone are evenly distributed throughout the cross-section of the bone, but in other mammals the osteons tend to be aligned in horizontal layers. The bones of large mammals are also denser and feel heavier compared to human bones of the same size, and the bones of animals that run on four legs tend to have strongly grooved surfaces where the limb bones fit together at the joints. Isolated fragments of bones and teeth can easily be misidentified, fragmentary human bones sometimes being confused with those of large carnivores such as bears. Fragments of the limb bones of large birds such as swans or geese are also occasionally mistaken for human remains. The bones of the human skull vault can be distinguished from those of other mammals by their double layers of compact bone which are separated by a layer of spongy bone. The inner surface of the human cranial vault is also distinguished by the presence of a branching network of grooves for the blood vessels.

Child or adult?

Once the skeletal remains are confidently identified as human, small size is obviously the chief factor that distinguishes the skeletons of children. The bones of children are also of different proportions and the shafts of their long bones are not yet attached to the joint-bearing ends of the bones (the epiphyses). The bones of infants are thin and porous and the epiphyses, which are quite small, may be missing. In the skeletons of newborns the skull bones are very thin and fragile and have 'feathered' edges. The bones of the base of the skull and the face and jaws are diminutive compared to the cranial vault because the brain is already well developed at birth. The long bones of the arms and legs in the newborn are

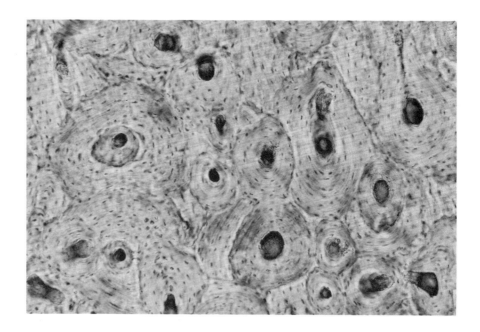

1 A thin section of human bone, viewed under phase contrast light (*top*) and polarising light (*bottom*). The field width in each picture is approximately 1.5 mm. Under phase contrast light, the osteons are visible as concentric layers of bone which contain small flat spaces once occupied by bone cells (osteocytes). The central Haversian canals, which appear as dark circular structures surrounded by the osteons, are about 50 microns in diameter. In the bottom illustration, polarised light accentuates the layers (lamellae) in human bone. Most of the thin section is occupied by the concentric lamellae of the osteons, which show a characteristic 'Maltese cross' pattern under polarised light. Between the osteons are small areas of the original circumferential lamellar bone that was present before the osteons were formed (*arrows*).

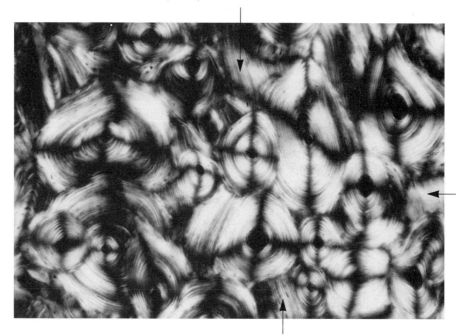

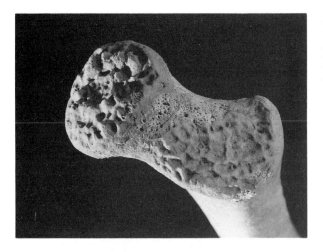

2 Bone surface underlying the cartilaginous growth plates on the head of the left femur of a seven-year-old child. The undulating or 'billowed' texture is characteristic of the growing ends of subadult human bones.

about the same size as an adult's palm bones (metacarpals), and because children of this age are growing rapidly the surfaces of their bones show patches of spongy new bone that have been deposited recently. In children's skeletons the ends of the long bones, which were overlain by the growth plates (layers of cartilage separating the epiphyses from the bone shaft), have a characteristic 'billowed' texture (fig. 2). The enamel surfaces of the milk teeth are already forming at birth, and are sometimes visible inside the jaws even though these teeth do not begin to emerge until the age of nine months. During childhood the cranial bones that enclose the brain progressively thicken, particularly along the suture lines where adjacent bones are joined together, and the skull takes on more adult proportions with rapid growth of the face and jaws. The growth in length of the long bones and the development of the teeth are the principal indicators of age at death in juveniles (fig. 3).

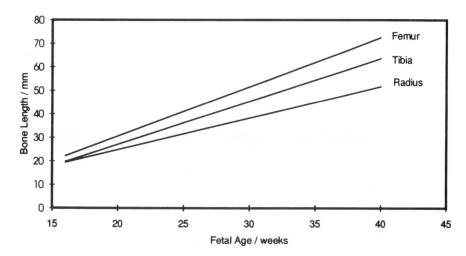

3 Graph showing the growth of the diaphyseal length of the femur, tibia and radius in human fetuses between 16 and 40 weeks after conception. The skeleton grows rapidly during the fetal stage and the first few months of post-natal life, and fetal age can be estimated to an accuracy of one or two weeks from measurements of long bone length.

Man or woman?

Male and female adult skeletons are different because there are sex differences in reproduction, growth rate and occupational behaviour. Differences directly relating to reproduction are found in the pelvis. The female pelvis (which includes the hip bones, sacrum and coccyx) is distinctive because it is adapted for child bearing. Although the female pelvis is less heavily built and has a smaller hip joint than the male, it is relatively wide. Compared to the male, the female pelvis is lower and broader. The joint surface between the hip bone and sacrum may be bordered by shallow grooves and the pubic bones are longer and the angle below them is more open (fig. **4**).

The bones of adult males are on average larger and heavier than those of adult females, although there is considerable overlap between the male and female ranges of variation. The differences between the sexes are especially noticeable in the diameters of the bone surfaces that underlie the joints, in the prominence of areas on bones where muscles are attached, and in the size of the teeth. However, only small differences exist between male and female skeletons before the onset of puberty, so it is very difficult to determine the sex of children's bones.

Sex differences are also noticeable in the skull. Males tend to have more prominent ridges where the muscles that move the head and lower jaw are

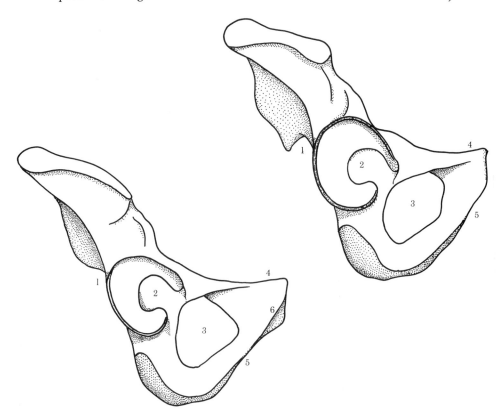

4 Hip bones of an adult female (*left*) and adult male (*right*) showing features that are useful for distinguishing the sexes. The female hip bone has a broader sciatic notch (**1**), smaller acetabulum (**2**), triangular-shaped obturator foramen (**3**), elongated pubic bone (**4**), wider and more concave subpubic angle (**5**) and a ventral arc (**6**).

10

Table 1 *Measurements useful in the determination of sex from adult limb bones*

	females	males
Scapula (length of glenoid cavity)	< 26	> 28
Humerus (vertical diameter of head)	< 43	> 47
Radius (maximum diameter of head)	< 21	> 24
Radius (distal transverse diameter)	< 33	> 36
Femur (vertical head diameter)	< 43	> 48
Femur (bicondylar breadth)	< 72	> 78

The measurements (in millimetres) in the left-hand column are the values below which the bone can confidently be assigned to the female sex. The measurements in the right-hand column indicate the values above which the bone can be assigned to the male sex. Intermediate values that fall between the female and male values cannot be assigned to either sex.

attached. These areas include the temporal lines, which curve across the sides of the skull where the temporalis muscle is attached, and the mastoid processes, which project downwards on the sides of the skull behind the ear holes. The neck muscle attachment area at the rear of the skull, the cheek bones, and the angle of the lower jaw are also more prominent in males. However, these muscle attachments may also be prominent in women who have habitually prepared animal skins with their teeth or carried heavy loads on their heads. The joint surfaces of the skull are larger in males, as are the average dimensions of the face, upper jaw and teeth. The brow ridges are more prominent in males, who also tend to have a well-developed bony chin.

Apart from the bones of the pelvis, the sex differences in the arm and leg bones are mainly in overall size and ruggedness. The dimensions of joint surfaces allow reasonable differentiation between the sexes, but there is a substantial zone of overlap and only individuals whose measurements lie above or below this zone can be attributed with confidence (Table 1).

Discriminant function analysis is a method that allows several measurements to be combined in a single function that best discriminates between two collections of bones of similar type, e.g. two groups of skulls. In forensic anthropology, which deals with human remains of recent origin, the method is used to determine the sex and population relationships of unidentified skeletal remains. In combining different measurements the discriminant function gives more weight to the variables that are most effective in distinguishing between the groups. Discriminant functions have been calculated for determining sex from measurements of the cranium, mandible, pelvis and other regions of the skeleton. The functions are specific to particular populations, and it is not known whether they give accurate results for archaeological skeletons.

Cremations

Cremated human bone, even when extremely fragmented, can provide valuable data both about the individual and about the conditions under which cremation occurred. Archaeological cremations usually contain between 200 and 2000 g of skeletal material, of which skull fragments average 20 per cent of the total. The colour and condition of the bone fragments give an indication of the temperature, duration and oxidising conditions under which cremation occurred. Bones that are subjected to sustained temperatures above 650°C show a white or grey color-

5 Human bone from a Bronze Age cremation. The bone fragments show heat cracking, distortion and shrinkage resulting from prolonged burning at a high temperature.

ation, and the outer surfaces of the fragments may have a glassy appearance indicating recrystallisation of the mineral portion of the bone. At firing temperatures above 900°C all organic components of bone are burnt off, and weight loss of more than 40 per cent occurs. High temperatures also result in distortion and shrinkage in linear dimensions, so measurements taken on cremated bones may underestimate the true dimensions of the bones. Warping and twisting of long bones, accompanied by curved transverse cracking, may confirm that cremation was performed when the bones were 'green' or flesh-covered, rather than dry or after the flesh had been removed (fig. **5**).

— 2 —

The Evidence for Age and Population Structure

The determination of demographic characteristics from skeletal remains is one of the more important tasks of the skeletal biologist. In many societies, both past and present, the funerary ritual differs according to the age, sex and status of the deceased. Independent biological determination of the age of a skeleton contributes to an understanding of the cultural distinctions between individual burials, while the age structure of a cemetery population can also provide information about fertility and mortality among the 'contributing' population or community served by the cemetery.

Growth and ageing

Growth and age changes in bone

Methods of ageing human skeletons have been developed by forensic anthropologists and archaeologists concerned with identifying human remains of recent origin. Some of these methods are applied to archaeological remains, although differences between populations and the influence of changes in diet and occupational activities may reduce the accuracy of these methods when they are applied to past peoples.

Although the skeletons of children are often less well preserved than those of adults, it is relatively easy to estimate their age at death. Growth and maturation of a child's skeleton follows a sequence that, at least in the early years of life, is fairly predictable in its timing. The bones of the skeleton first begin to ossify in the developing embryo long before birth, in the eighth week after conception. The enamel of the milk teeth also begins to form before birth in the second trimester of pregnancy, between twelve and sixteen weeks after conception. The milk teeth usually start to erupt through the gum when the infant is nine months old.

The rate of growth of the skeleton is most rapid during the fetal and early post-natal period. The long bones of the limbs increase in length through the addition of bone at the growth plates, which are layers of cartilage that separate the epiphyses (joint-bearing ends of the bone) from the diaphyses or bone shafts. The average rates of growth of the long bones have been determined for present-day children and for prehistoric children whose age has been estimated from the development of their teeth (see below). When the resulting charts are compared (fig. **6**), considerable differences in age-specific bone length are seen between modern and ancient populations, past populations showing slower rates of bone growth.

At the end of puberty the bones stop growing and the growth plates ossify, so that the epiphyses become fused to the shaft of the bone. The ages at which particular epiphyses become fused is predictable, and can be used to estimate age at death in children and young adults (Table 2).

The skeleton, like other parts of the body, is subject to 'wear and tear' and the resulting changes with age in adult bones are measurable, although they do not proceed on such a regular basis as the developmental changes that occur in children. Regular, cumulative changes occur in the microstructure of the compact cortical bone that forms the shafts of long bones such as the femur. Osteons are visible in thin, transparent cross-sections of adult cortical bone (fig. **1**). They are concentric layers of bone surrounding a narrow canal and are produced by a natural process called remodelling, in which bone is continually removed and replaced in response to changes in loading and mechanical stress. The bones of young adults contain relatively few osteons, but as remodelling progresses over a period of years the number of osteons visible in microscopic cross-sections of bone gradually increases. This process can be applied as a method for determining age at death of adult archaeological skeletons.

At the front of the pelvis the two hip bones are linked by a fibrocartilaginous joint called the pubic symphysis. In young adults the surface of the bone underlying this joint has a distinctive appearance, with about eight horizontal ridges and intervening deep grooves crossing the surface from front to back. In older individuals the appearance of the pubic symphyseal surface is modified through the normal stresses acting on the joint. The transverse ridges become less well defined as the grooves are filled in with new bone, while the front and rear margins become thickened. Eventually these margins join to form a rim around the symphyseal surface. In the oldest age categories the entire surface becomes

Table 2 Ages at which the growth centres (epiphyses) and centres of ossification unite in the skeletons of children and young adults

0–9 months	Greater wing of sphenoid fuses to body of sphenoid
6–9 months	Mandibular symphysis fuses
0–12 months	Vertebral arches fuse in the midline
1–2 years	Frontal bone fuses along metopic suture in the midline
2–3 years	Lateral part of occipital bone fuses to basioccipital
3–4 years	Vertebral arches fuse to vertebral bodies in the cervical vertebrae
4–5 years	Greater tubercle fuses to the head of the humerus
5–6 years	Vertebral arches fuse to vertebral bodies in the lumbar vertebrae
6–8 years	Inferior pubic ramus fuses to ischial ramus on the hip bone
13–15 years	Ilium, ischium and pubis fuse to form the hip bone
14–15 years	Distal epiphysis fuses on the humerus
15–16 years	Proximal epiphysis on radius and epiphyses on metacarpals fuse
17–18 years	Proximal and distal epiphyses fuse on femur
18–19 years	Iliac crest fuses on the hip bone
19–20 years	Head of humerus fuses
25–28 years	Sternal end of clavicle fuses

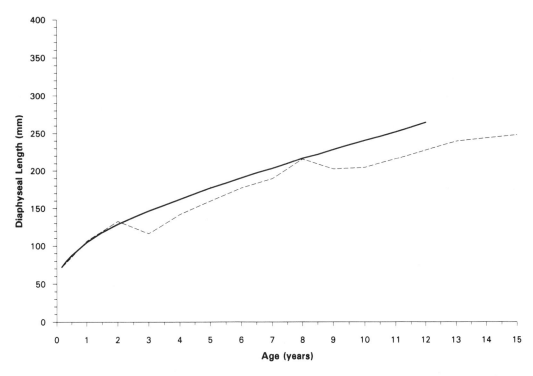

6 Graphs of the diaphyseal length of the humerus (*above*) and the femur (*below*) in modern children (solid line) and in tenth-century Anglo–Saxon children (dashed line). Note that at all stages of growth the bones were shorter in the Anglo–Saxon children.

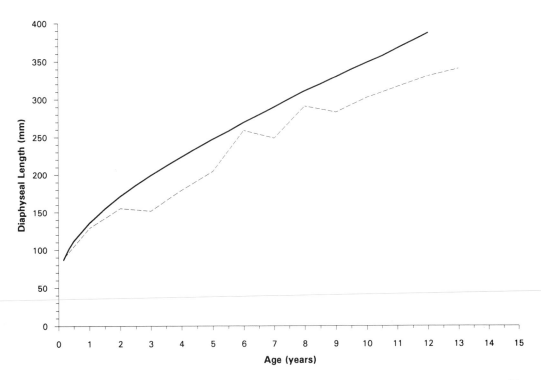

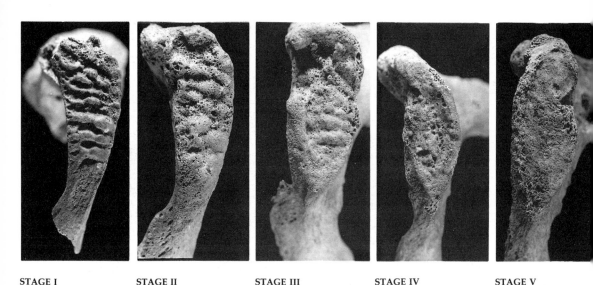

STAGE I STAGE II STAGE III STAGE IV STAGE V

7 Stages of age-related change on the medial surface of the pubic symphysis. Approximate age ranges in years for each stage for males (**m**) and females (**f**) are as follows: STAGE I: **m:** 15–20/**f:** 15–20; STAGE II: **m:** 20–5/**f:** 20–30; STAGE III: **m:** 20–35/**f:** 25–40; STAGE IV: **m:** 25–45/**f:** 25–50; STAGE V: **m:** 35–55/**f:** 35–65. Note that the error in age determination increases in the higher stages.

pitted and porous, and has an irregularly uneven appearance (fig. 7). The typical appearance of the symphyseal surface at different ages has been determined separately for human male and female skeletons of known age, allowing the estimation of age at death in skeletons from archaeological and forensic contexts.

Development and wear of the teeth

Dental development provides one of the most reliable means of determining age at death in children's skeletons. Each tooth consists of a crown and root which form within the jaw; when the tooth crown is completed it emerges through the gum as the root is developing. Stages of tooth development can be recognised either by visual inspection or from an X-ray image of the jaw. The final stage of growth before full adulthood is the emergence of the last of the molar teeth at the back of the jaw, the so-called 'wisdom teeth' (fig. 8).

Cementum is a thin layer of bone-like tissue that surrounds the roots of a tooth, anchoring it through fine ligaments to the adjacent bone of the tooth socket. The cementum can be seen on isolated teeth as a white material that contrasts with the yellow colour of the root dentine. Cementum is continually deposited during adult life and is rarely modified or resorbed unless the tooth becomes diseased. Microscopic cross-sections of cementum show that the tissue is made up of alternating light and dark bands which correspond to seasonal variation in growth: the darker bands are formed during the winter season. By counting the number of light or dark cycles, and then adding this number to the age at formation of the tooth root, the age at death of the individual can be determined.

As soon as teeth have fully erupted into the mouth they begin to wear down, partly from abrasive particles in the diet but also from contact between the teeth

16

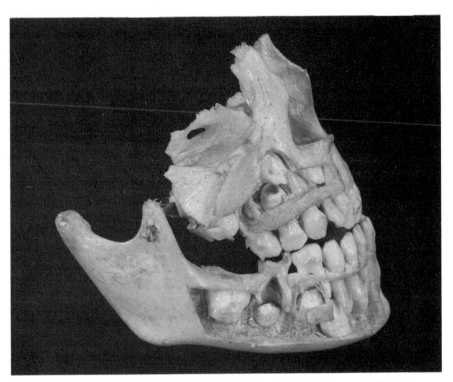

8 Upper and lower jaws of a five-year-old child in which the deciduous or 'milk' teeth have all erupted. The bone has been removed from the sides of the jaws to show the crowns of the developing permanent teeth, which lie just under the roots of the deciduous teeth.

in opposite jaws and from the non-dietary usage of teeth as 'tools'. The pattern and rate of dental wear is influenced by cultural practices and by the incidence of dental disease, because the loss of teeth through decay, injury or periodontal disease may increase the loading and therefore the rate of wear on the remaining healthy teeth. Because both dental disease and cultural practices vary between populations, it is expected that rates of dental wear will also differ between groups. Nevertheless, for a particular individual the rate of dental wear can be assessed by determining the gradient of wear along the tooth row. In an adult jaw, in which the permanent molars will have erupted at approximately six-year intervals, there will be most wear on the first molar, less on the second molar and least on the third. The difference in wear between the first and second molar, and between the second and third, is thus a measure of the amount of wear that occurs on molar teeth in about six years. This allows the investigator to assess whether the individual belongs to a population with characteristically high or low rates of dental wear (fig. **9**).

The degree of dental wear in archaeological skeletons can be compared with wear stages in skeletons of known age, thereby allowing an estimate of age at death to be obtained for archaeological material. Ageing by dental wear is considered to be less reliable than pubic symphysis ageing, but age estimates obtained in this way can be combined with estimates from other methods in order to improve the accuracy. Other commonly used macroscopic ageing methods in-

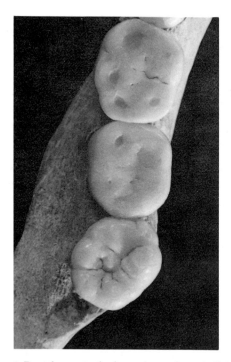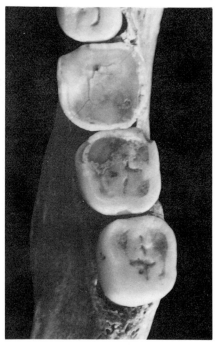

9 Dental wear in the lower jaws of two individuals of different ages. (*left*) Age approximately 18 years. Wear has exposed several small areas of dentine (darker in colour than the surrounding enamel) on the chewing surface of the first molar tooth (*top*). The second molar tooth, which emerges from the gum about six years later than the first molar, has less wear and shows only a single small area of exposed dentine. The third molar, or 'wisdom tooth', is almost unworn. (*right*) Age approximately 40–50 years. Wear on the first molar (*top*) has completely removed the surface enamel apart from a thin rim around the outside of the tooth. Large areas of dentine are also exposed on the wearing surfaces of the second and third molars.

clude the fusion of the sutures along which the bones of the skull are joined, changes in the internal structure of the heads of the humerus and femur (observable on X-rays of the bones) and changes in the appearance of bone underlying the sacro-iliac joint on the hip bone. Sometimes the estimation of age at death for individual skeletons in a large sample can be improved through seriation. This involves placing all the specimens in a rank order series, according to one or more of the ageing criteria employed, so that each individual can be compared with other individuals of similar age at death. Only when the investigator is sure of the rank order are the skeletons then grouped into different age categories.

Palaeodemography

Palaeodemography is the study of population size, structure, density and dynamics in earlier human societies. We have now become accustomed to a rapid increase in population numbers, but in the past populations were often limited by the carrying capacity of the land as well as by famine, warfare and disease epidemics. Estimates of population size for past societies, especially prehistoric communities, can at best be only approximate, but the distribution of age-at-death in samples of skeletal remains can be used, with some reservations, to investigate population structure and patterns of mortality. Palaeodemography focuses on mortality because rates of fertility and patterns of migration are highly culture-dependent and often unknown. As it is difficult to determine the sex of children's skeletons, palaeodemographic analysis is usually carried out on samples in which the sexes are combined.

The proportion of people dying each year within a population is known as the crude mortality rate. This crude rate masks important differences in age-specific mortality: in virtually all populations there is a much higher risk of dying among the very young and the very old, and the age-specific mortality therefore follows a U-shaped curve (fig. 10). Another way of representing age-specific mortality data is on a survivorship curve, which shows the decline in the number of individuals surviving at successive age intervals out of a theoretical group of one hundred individuals born in the same year (such a group is called a 'cohort'). High infant mortality is shown by a steep drop in the numbers surviving through the earliest age intervals. Lower mortality in middle life is indicated by the shallower gradient of the curve in this region, while the curve steepens again in the highest age categories to reflect raised mortality rates in the aged.

Age-specific mortality and survivorship curves follow well-defined patterns for all known human populations, and the greatest differences between populations occur in rates of infant mortality, which are the main determinants of average life expectancy. A population in which the birth rate is equal to the death rate, and for which there is no net immigration or emigration, is called a stationary population. Under these circumstances a more or less constant number of

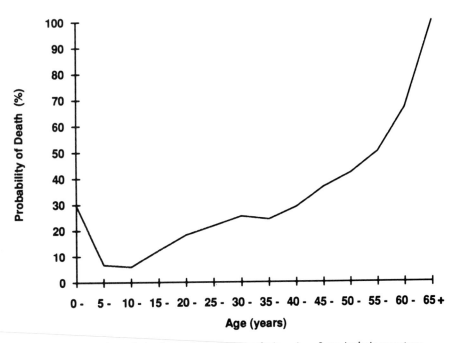

10 Mortality curve for a skeletal sample from a North American Late Archaic cemetery site. The curve shows the probability of death at five-year age intervals and has the U-shape that is also characteristic of the mortality curves of modern populations. The probability of death in this sample is high in the period immediately following birth, declines to a minimum at ten years of age and then steadily increases during adulthood.

deaths will occur in each age interval each year, and a random sample of deaths spread over several years (such as is approximated by a cemetery 'population') will give an accurate estimation of age-specific mortality. This type of calculation depends on the assumption that a series of individuals buried in a cemetery is an unbiased sample of the deaths occurring in the community served by the cemetery. The three main confounding factors are, first, that individuals may die elsewhere (for example in warfare) or be excluded from the cemetery for other reasons (very young infants, criminals and suicides may all be buried in other locations); second, population growth or decline, which if continued throughout the use period of the cemetery will influence the age structure of the sample; and third, inaccuracies in anthropological methods of skeletal age determination.

If the population is growing throughout the period represented by the skeletal sample, and if this growth is caused by the birth rate exceeding the death rate (rather than by net immigration), the number of deaths in the youngest age categories will be increased relative to those in the oldest categories because they are 'fed' by expanded numbers of young people in the population. The effect on survivorship curves of a population growth rate of one per cent per year (a value typical of present-day developing countries) is shown in figure 11. In practice, cemeteries usually serve well-defined local communities and population growth may be accommodated by migration to new settlements, so the 'contributing population' may be static despite a general increase in population numbers.

Methods of age determination are much more accurate for juvenile skeletal remains than for those of adults. It may prove impossible even to estimate the age of fragmentary and incomplete adult skeletons, yet if these individuals are omitted from the analysis the rates of adult age-specific mortality will be underestimated. Adult skeletons of unknown age can be distributed across the adult age categories in proportion to the number of aged adults in each category. More difficult to control for is the under-representation of children, which has the effect of underestimating infant mortality and thus making the survivorship curve too shallow (fig. 12). A serious problem with many anthropological methods of adult age determination is that they underestimate age at death in the higher age categories. This is instantly recognisable in survivorship curves that decline to a value of zero before reaching age categories above sixty (fig. 13). All known living populations, even those with very high crude mortality and low life expectancy, have a proportion of individuals surviving into their eighties and nineties.

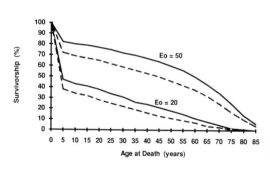

11 Effect of population growth on survivorship curves. The survivorship curves (solid lines) show the percentage of survivors, at successive intervals of five years, out of a population of 100 individuals born in the same year. The upper curve shows survivorship in a group with relatively low mortality and a life expectancy at birth of 50 years (E_0 = 50). The lower curve shows survivorship in a group with high mortality and a life expectancy at birth of 20 years (E_0 = 20). The effect of a rate of population growth of 1% per year is to depress the survivorship curves to the values given by the dashed lines, with an apparent lowering of life expectancy. Intrinsic population growth (i.e. population expansion that is birth-linked rather than migration-linked) effectively increases the proportion of young individuals in the population, leading to higher infant mortality and decreased average life expectancy.

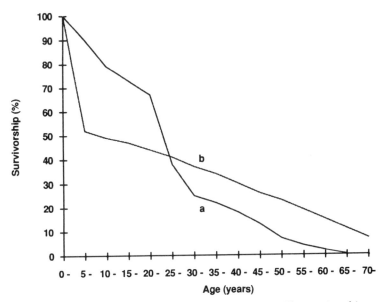

12 Effect of infant under-representation on a survivorship curve. The survivorship calculated from the ages at death of skeletons from the medieval cemetery of St Helen on the Walls, York (**a**) is compared with the survivorship curve from a model life table population with the same life expectancy at birth, $E_0 = 25$ years (**b**). Under-representation of infants in the archaeological sample leads to a much shallower initial slope to the survivorship curve compared to the curve for the model life table population.

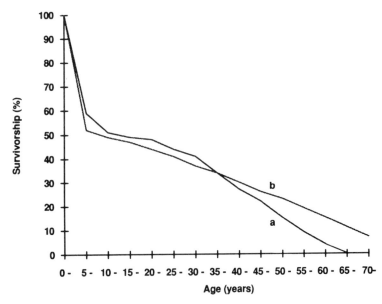

13 Effect of under-aging of adults on a survivorship curve. The survivorship curve calculated from the ages at death of skeletons from a cemetery on the Isle of Ensay, Scotland (**a**) is compared with a model life table survivorship curve (**b**). Up to the age of 30 years, the curve for the Ensay population closely parallels the standard life table curve. After age 30 the curve for the Ensay skeletal sample declines more rapidly, suggesting that the ages at death of the older adult skeletons may have been systematically underestimated.

Chemical and Biomolecular Evidence

Trace elements

The major chemical elements of bone are those of the mineral phase (calcium, phosphorus, oxygen) and the organic phase (carbon, nitrogen, hydrogen, oxygen). These elements can be measured by standard chemical methods, and the nitrogen concentration, which reflects the protein content of bone, is sometimes used as a measure of the amount of loss of organic material from bone that has been buried in the ground. Other chemical elements are present in bone in trace amounts and are therefore referred to as 'trace elements' (Table 3). Some trace elements are essential for the normal function of the body – these include copper, manganese, zinc and iodine (a deficiency of iodine causes goitre, a disease of the thyroid glands). Other elements that are present in bone are non-essential or even toxic, such as lead, mercury and arsenic.

The amount of a particular trace element that is taken into the body depends on the amount present in the diet, as well as the extent of ingestion via other routes such as inhalation or absorption through the skin. Trace elements such as strontium and lead that have physicochemical properties similar to calcium become concentrated in the bones and teeth, where they may be retained throughout life. After burial, however, some elements can move between bone and the surrounding soil or vice versa, the element's mobility depending on soil chemistry, ground water acidity and the length of time that the bone has been buried. Zinc and barium are relatively immobile, but lead will migrate from soil to

Table 3 Trace elements in human bone (normal levels are given as parts per million of bone ash)

Essential		Non-essential or toxic	
Copper	25	Aluminium	1–10
Iodine	< 1	Arsenic	0–5
Iron	500	Barium	10–20
Manganese	10	Lead	< 70
Zinc	200	Mercury	< 1
		Strontium	100–200

bone, particularly in acidic soils. The concentrations of trace elements in the adult teeth generally reflect the amounts absorbed into the body during childhood because, unlike bone, teeth are not remodelled. Teeth can, however, absorb elements from fluids in the mouth, as shown by the uptake of fluorine from toothpaste and fluoridated water (offering protection against tooth decay).

Because of their low concentration, special methods are used to detect and measure the amounts of trace elements in biological materials. The spectroscopic methods of atomic absorption (AAS) and emission spectroscopy (ES) use high-energy flame or plasma sources to excite the atoms in a sample. Each chemical element will absorb and emit light of specific wavelengths and the intensity of this light can be measured by detectors. A related method called X-ray fluorescence (XRF) uses a beam of particles to excite the atoms in the sample. The characteristic frequencies of X-rays given off by the atoms are measured and used to calculate the concentrations of particular elements. In neutron activation analysis (NAA) the sample is irradiated by exposure to neutrons in a nuclear reactor. This renders some atoms unstable (i.e. radioactive) and when these atoms subsequently decay, the pattern of expelled energy in the form of photons, electrons and alpha particles is characteristic of each element. Mass spectrometry is a highly sensitive method of analysis in which atoms are ionised and their atomic weight determined. It is the method by which the proportions of stable isotopes in a sample can be determined (see below). The results of all the above methods are usually presented as parts per million (ppm) of dry bone or of bone ash. In archaeological bone an unknown amount of the organic phase may have been lost, so the concentration is best expressed in terms of bone ash weight.

Strontium is of particular value in studies of past diets because animals, including humans, selectively absorb more calcium than strontium from their diets. At each level in the food chain the ratio of calcium to strontium (Ca/Sr) in animal tissues is increased by up to a factor of five. Most groups of humans consume an omnivorous diet and their bones are therefore intermediate between herbivores and carnivores in their Ca/Sr ratio. The proportion of meat to vegetable foodstuffs in the diet will influence the position of human Ca/Sr ratios compared to other animals. The pattern is complicated, however, by particular foods that have anomalous strontium content. Some shellfish concentrate strontium, while dairy products such as milk, cheese and yoghurt are depleted in strontium compared to meat from the same animal.

Intake of the toxic element lead is associated with industrial production of the metal (total world industrial output now exceeds one million tonnes per year). Lead is absorbed from food, drink and respired particles such as cigarette smoke, and most of the lead that is retained in the body is stored in the mineral compounds of bones and teeth. Archaeological skeletons from pre-metallurgical populations of Peru have concentrations of about 1 ppm ash weight, but typical bone lead concentrations in modern industrial societies are about 40 ppm ash weight, higher levels being found in males and in older individuals. Much higher concentrations are often found in the bones of individuals who used pewter cooking and eating utensils (pewter is an alloy containing lead and zinc). Analysis of lead in archaeological skeletons has demonstrated differences between high-status plantation owners and low-status slaves in the North American colonial period. The pewter-using plantation owners had average skeletal lead concentrations of 185 ppm ash weight, compared to an average of 35 ppm in the slaves, who probably used earthenware cooking and eating utensils.

Stable isotopes

Isotopes are different forms of an element that have the same number of electrons and protons but different numbers of neutrons. Because the chemical properties of an element are determined largely by its atomic number (i.e. number of electrons and protons), different isotopes of an element are very similar chemically but have slightly different physical properties due to differences in their atomic mass. Many isotopes are unstable and are subject to radioactive decay (for example, the isotope carbon-14), but the elements nitrogen and carbon have stable isotopes that occur naturally throughout the environment. Living organisms obtain most of their nitrogen and carbon from the atmosphere, in which the ratios of the stable isotopes of nitrogen (^{14}N and ^{15}N) and those of carbon (^{12}C and ^{13}C) are relatively constant. When plants absorb carbon dioxide, the heavier isotope ^{13}C diffuses more slowly and the concentration of this isotope in the plant (when expressed as a ratio to the more common isotope ^{12}C) is therefore depleted compared to the ratio in the atmosphere. Certain types of plants have different photosynthetic mechanisms and as a result their $^{13}C/^{12}C$ ratios are distinguishable. Animals that feed predominantly on one type of plant will also show a characteristic $^{13}C/^{12}C$ ratio in the carbon contained in the organic part of their skeletons. In archaeological research the $^{13}C/^{12}C$ ratio in human bone has been used to detect the onset of maize agriculture in the New World.

The ratio of the stable nitrogen isotopes ^{14}N and ^{15}N changes at each step (trophic level) in the food chain, because when protein is consumed some amino acids are metabolised and the lighter isotope ^{14}N is excreted more quickly in the urine. Thus ^{15}N accumulates relative to ^{14}N at each trophic level and animals at the top of the food chain, such as marine carnivores, have the highest $^{15}N/^{14}N$ ratios. Analysis of nitrogen isotopes in collagen extracted from archaeological human bone can therefore give an indication of diet. Analyses of collagen from the skeleton of a Neanderthal are reported to show that the hominid had a diet intermediate in animal protein content between the diets of a wolf and a fox. Similar studies of a fossil human relative, *Australopithecus robustus*, show that this early hominid had an omnivorous diet.

Detection and characterisation of biomolecules

Ancient bone contains a range of organic molecules including proteins, lipids and nucleic acids. These molecules are large, complex and highly specific at the species, population and even individual level. They have great potential use in the investigation of the origins and diversity of past human populations.

The major structural protein in mature bone is collagen, but bone also contains a variety of other proteins, some of which are present in the blood. Albumin and haemoglobin are the two most common blood proteins present in bone, and the small amounts present in archaeological skeletons can be detected by immunochemical methods. One of the most sensitive and specific ways of detecting human proteins is an ELISA method based on a monoclonal antibody (ELISA stands for enzyme-linked immunosorbent assay). Monoclonal antibodies have the ability to recognise a particular point in a protein molecule and are therefore less likely to react with different molecules, such as other proteins or the same protein from a different species of animal. ELISA assays, which can detect human albumin at concentrations as low as one part in five hundred, have shown that intact albumin survives in human bone up to four thousand years old, as well as in bone that has been cremated. These methods have also detected the presence of human albumin in red pigments used in Palaeolithic rock art, and have possibly shown the species of origin of blood residues on the surface of stone tools.

The nucleic acids DNA and RNA are biological molecules carrying the genetic information that controls the structure, development and metabolism of an organism. DNA can be extracted from ancient bone, but it tends to be broken into short fragments. Within the nucleus of a living cell DNA is relatively stable, but after death some damage and loss of DNA occur through chemical processes such as oxidation and enzymatic degradation. The newly developed method of polymerase chain reaction (PCR) can be used to 'amplify' measurable quantities of DNA, starting from extremely small amounts, even when the DNA is slightly damaged.

PCR has been used to amplify DNA extracted from brain tissue preserved in 7500-year-old human skeletons from Windover in Florida. The DNA contained parts of the HLA (human lymphocyte antigen) family of genes, which can provide information about population and familial relationships. In another experiment, a short sequence from the human Y-chromosome was detected in DNA extracted from archaeological human bone. Because genes specific to the Y-chromosome are present only in male individuals, this method may be useful in determining the sex of unidentified human skeletal remains.

— 4 —

Diseases and Disorders

Our knowledge about disease in earlier peoples comes from the study of literary sources and artistic representations (paintings and sculptures) and from the analysis of skeletal remains, mummies and other preserved tissues. Preserved human remains are the only source of evidence prior to the development of art and writing, but it is clear that even the earliest humans must have suffered from many of the diseases that afflict modern populations. Several examples are known of skeletons of individuals dating from Palaeolithic times who survived to an advanced age despite having severely disabling illnesses that would have reduced their ability to carry out subsistence activities.

In ancient Egypt descriptions of medical conditions and their treatment were recorded on papyri, and the existence of a range of diseases has been demonstrated through the careful study of mummified tissues. In addition to diseases of the bones and teeth, Egyptian mummies show evidence of parasitic diseases (including bilharzia and tapeworm), gall and kidney stones, hardening of the arteries and infectious diseases such as smallpox and leprosy (fig. **14**). The adoption of agriculture, which spread through Europe between about 8000 and 3000 years ago and led to increased population sizes and the development of settled communities, is thought to have promoted an increase in the incidence of infectious diseases. The bacteria responsible for tuberculosis and plague, for example, are harboured by animals associated with human settlements; with the development of long-distance contact and trade these diseases would have spread more easily. In some societies agriculture also led to over-dependence on a single harvested food resource, resulting in nutritional imbalance and deficiencies of essential vitamins. Early agricultural communities would have suffered from many of the bacterial diseases seen in present-day communities, but many viral infections are of more recent origin. Infections such as measles, whooping cough and poliomyelitis persist only in dense population clusters that sustain a high frequency of interpersonal contact.

The tradition of medical intervention developed in the classical Greek and Roman world was lost in western Europe following the collapse of the Roman empire. Ill health was explained by supernatural causes, and healing centred on prayers and repentance, assisted by herbal remedies. The modern tradition of

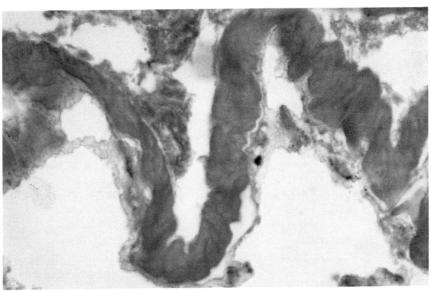

14 Microscopic section through the wall of a hydatid cyst in an Egyptian mummy. The cyst contained larvae of the tapeworm *Echinococcus*. Hydatid cysts develop slowly over several years but can eventually grow to several centimetres in diameter.

institutionalised care of the sick and disabled became common in western Europe only in later medieval times. Most medieval hospitals fall into the categories of leper houses, almshouses and hospices (caring for poor wayfarers and pilgrims); there were relatively few institutions that cared for general sickness in a manner analogous to modern general hospitals. Medieval hospitals were closely linked to the Christian church, and in the case of leprosy hospitals would usually possess their own chapels and burial grounds.

Of course, many diseases do not leave their mark on the bones and teeth. People recover quickly from mild infections and superficial injuries which leave no impression on the skeleton, whereas some of the fatal diseases common in the past, such as plague and cholera, killed their victims so quickly that skeletal changes did not have time to appear. The most common disorders seen in human skeletons are healed bone fractures, chronic joint diseases, chronic infections of bone and dental diseases such as caries and periodontal disease.

Skeletal disorders

Trauma
Like all rigid materials, a bone will break (fracture) when sufficient force is applied to it. The way in which a bone breaks depends on the direction of the force and on whether the force compresses, bends or twists the bone (when placed under tension, bone is normally stronger than adjacent tissues, so high tensile forces will dislocate joints rather than fracture bones). Fractures may also occur during normal activities if a bone has become weakened by osteoporosis, infection or the growth of a tumour.

Fractures of bone that occurred at or around the time of death may be difficult to recognise in archaeological skeletons, but if the individual survived for some time after injury the fracture will show signs of the natural remodelling and repair process that all bones (but not teeth) undergo in response to trauma. Repair begins with the formation of fibrous tissue that binds together the main bone fragments. Smaller bone fragments are removed by bone cells, and new bone mineral is then deposited around the fibrous tissue to form a bony callus that encloses the site of the fracture. This callus, which reaches its maximum size four to six weeks after the injury, is then remodelled over a period of several months, eventually restoring the original strength and rigidity of the bone. Immobilisation of the affected bone is important in the healing process: movement between the broken parts will delay ossification, or even result in a fibrocartilaginous connection developing instead of bony union. Well-healed fractures show a continuous, smooth join between the broken pieces, but there is often some shortening or deformity of the bone as a result of poor alignment of the broken ends.

If the skin has been broken through by penetration of a sharp object, such as a projectile or by the broken end of the bone itself, the fracture site may become infected and the bone will show signs of inflammation as in periostitis and osteomyelitis (see below). Fractures that cause shortening and deformity of the bone can lead to abnormal stresses being placed on adjacent joints, with the subsequent development of degenerative joint disease.

The distribution of fractures in different parts of the skeleton, as well as the overall frequency of trauma in a skeletal population, provides some indication of cause. Fractures of the skull and of the middle part of the bones of the forearm are characteristic of interpersonal physical violence, often involving weapons. Because the majority of individuals are right-handed, such fractures tend to be inflicted more frequently on the left side of the victim's body. Fractures of the neck of the femur, of the wrist and of the lower leg, as well as compression fractures of the vertebrae, are normally caused by accidental rather than deliber-

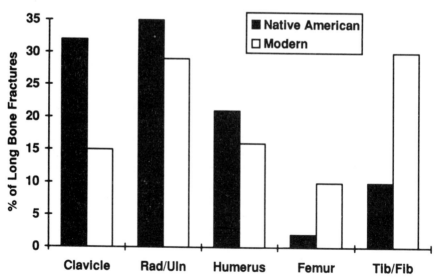

15 Distribution of fractures of the long bones in archaeological samples of Native Americans and in a twentieth-century hospital population. In the modern population fractures of the leg bones occur more frequently, while those of the shoulder and arm bones are less common.

ate injury. Fractures of the femur were uncommon in prehistoric populations, but increased in frequency in historical times with the development of more rapid forms of transport (fig. **15**).

Dislocations can be detected if the separation between the bones occurred some time before death and the injury was not subsequently corrected through treatment. Dislocations of the hip and shoulder joints are the most difficult to treat, and are therefore the most likely to give rise to pathological changes in the bones. Dislocation of the hip is not necessarily traumatic, as it can be present at birth as a congenital disease (see below). Chronic dislocation of the hip is characterised by flattening of the normally spherical head of the femur, and by shallowing of the socket on the hip bone with a secondary joint forming behind or below the original joint. In dislocation of the shoulder a new joint surface develops on the front aspect of the shoulder blade, while the original joint surface at the lateral end of the shoulder blade deteriorates.

Infections of bone
Infection of the human body by pathogenic organisms gives rise to inflammation, a cellular reaction with symptoms of pain, swelling and increased temperature. Some infective diseases can be recognised by the specific types and skeletal location of the bone lesions they cause. Other diseases produce non-specific changes, such as periostitis which is typical of several infections of bone.

Bone changes produced by infective organisms can be broadly classified as periostitis, affecting only the external surface of the bone, and osteomyelitis, which is a more deep-seated infection involving pus-forming bacteria. In periostitis the layer of tissue covering the bone reacts to the infection by forming a thin layer of woven bone that is deposited on top of the original bone cortex. Osteomyelitis mainly occurs in the tubular bones, where the bacteria invade the medullary cavity (the hollow space inside the shaft of the bone), producing destruction and cavitation of the surrounding bone, with irregular new bone formation that enlarges and deforms the original outline of the bone. The infection may be drained by a small hole (sinus) that connects the inside of the bone to the surrounding soft tissues.

Some infectious diseases that produce characteristic skeletal changes are leprosy, tuberculosis, treponemal disease (e.g. syphilis) and poliomyelitis. Leprosy is caused by chronic infection by the organism *Mycobacterium leprae*. The disease primarily affects the peripheral nervous system, causing loss of sensation which in turn leads to the individual suffering damage to those parts of the body that are most exposed to trauma and infection. The bacteria also invade the peripheral blood vessels, leading to loss of circulation and localised gangrene. Ulceration of the tissues of the face, nose and eyes can result in bony changes, including erosion of the margins of the nasal aperture, pitting and perforation of the palate and resorption of the tooth sockets of the upper jaw with eventual loss of the upper front teeth. Repeated injury and loss of circulation in the hands and feet lead to narrowing and eventual loss of the finger and toe bones, damage to the joints of the foot and periostitis spreading up the surfaces of the bones of the lower leg (fig. **16**).

The primary route of infection by tuberculosis is respiratory, but in some individuals the organism spreads to the bones and joints. The disease produces osteomyelitis in bone and septic arthritis, with eventual destruction and bony fusion, in affected joints. The most commonly affected region in the skeleton is

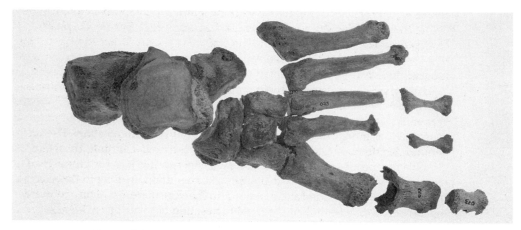

16 Bones of the left foot of a female skeleton from a medieval hospital cemetery in Grantham, Lincolnshire. Leprosy has caused the metatarsals to become narrowed or 'pencilled' towards their distal ends, and the phalanges are 'waisted' or narrowed in the middle. The disease has also damaged the joint of the great toe at the ball of the foot.

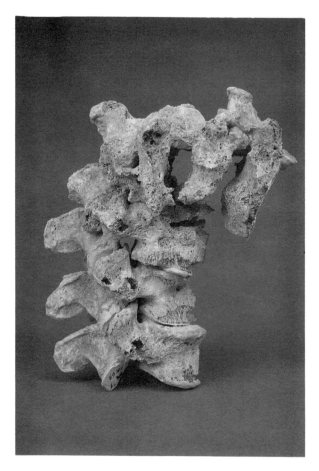

17 Tuberculosis of the spine in a young adult female Anglo–Saxon skeleton from Bedhampton, Hampshire.

the vertebral column in the lower part of the spine, where the infection destroys the vertebral bodies, leading to collapse and angular deformity (kyphosis, or 'hunchback') of the spinal column. The disease is usually localised to just a few vertebrae. Apart from the spine, the hip and knee joints are most commonly affected (fig. 17).

The treponemal diseases include venereal syphilis as well as the tropical diseases endemic syphilis, pinta and yaws. The infecting organism enters through the skin or mucous tissue, and bone changes occur only at a late stage in a minority of individuals, up to ten years after the initial infection. The most commonly affected skeletal sites are the bones of the cranial vault, the face and the tibia. Treponemal disease produces an osteomyelitis in which there is substantial bone destruction with active bone regeneration, leading to the affected bones becoming expanded and distorted. In the skull there are distinctive crater-like lesions on the frontal and parietal bones, and destruction of the nasal and palatal region (similar to leprosy). When the tibia is affected it becomes expanded and deformed in a forwards direction ('sabre shin'). Congenital syphilis occurs when an infected mother transmits the organism to her unborn child.

Poliomyelitis is a viral infection that can cause paralysis of the muscles. The disease, which usually occurs during childhood, may affect the growth of the skeleton because full muscular activity is essential for the normal development of bones. The bones from a paralysed limb are more slender than those of a normal limb and they have a smoother surface because the muscle attachments are less well developed.

Degenerative joint disease
Joints are complex structures that have a limited ability to repair damage caused either by normal wear or by disease. The identification of joint disease in archaeological skeletons depends on the recognition of the changes that occur on and adjacent to the smooth load-bearing surfaces of the bones. Both proliferation and destruction of bone can occur in joint disease. When a joint becomes damaged, new bone may be deposited at the margins of the joint (lipping) and at nearby insertions of ligaments and tendons. In severe cases bony outgrowths called osteophytes can be seen at the joint margin. Destruction of bone occurs through the formation of pitting (osteochondrosis) and by the development of cysts within the joint surface on the bone. When the articular cartilage within the joint has been destroyed, direct wear can occur between neighbouring bones, producing grooving and polishing (eburnation) of the bone's joint surfaces (fig. 18).

Arthritic complaints affect up to 40 per cent of adults in modern industrial populations, so it comes as no surprise that many skeletons from the past also show signs of joint degeneration. The most common joint disease in archaeological skeletons is osteoarthritis, in which degeneration of the articular cartilage results in narrowing of the joint space, lipping of the joint margins and pitting of the joint surface. The condition is most often found in the large weight-bearing joints of the hip, knee and spine. Other joints bearing large stresses, such as the temporomandibular joint where the lower jaw attaches to the cranium, are also frequently affected. Rheumatoid arthritis, which is rare in the archaeological record, is an erosive condition that affects mainly the joints of the hands and feet, although it can progressively involve other joints. Rheumatoid arthritis is more symmetrical in its distribution than osteoarthritis, and does not usually result in the fusion of adjacent bones.

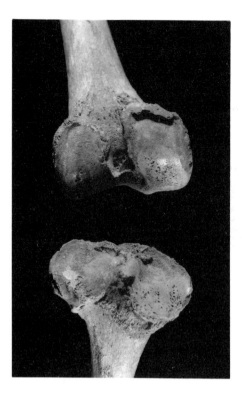

18 Arthritis of the knee joint. The medial condyle of the femur shows an area of polishing or eburnation where loss of the joint cartilage has allowed frictional contact between the bones of the femur and tibia. There is also the development of slight lipping around the margin of the joint surface.

Schmorl's nodes are circular or elongated depressions found on the upper and lower surfaces of the vertebral bodies. They are caused by extrusion of the fluid contents of intervertebral discs into the adjacent spongy bone of the vertebra, and may therefore reflect either increased physical stress or a weakening of the tissues of the vertebral disc or the underlying bone. Schmorl's nodes are very common, being found in up to 75 per cent of both modern and archaeological skeletons.

Metabolic, nutritional and deficiency diseases
The maintenance of normal bone structure depends on adequate nutrition and on the regulation of the circulating vitamins and hormones that influence bone cell activity. Bone is remodelled throughout life, with the rate of bone removal (resorption) normally balanced by an equivalent amount of new bone formation. If resorption exceeds bone formation the condition of osteoporosis develops, in which the compact layer on the outside of the bone is thinned and the underlying spongy bone becomes more porous. Post-menopausal women are particularly at risk of developing osteoporosis because of the decline in their production of oestrogen.

The main substances that control bone growth and maturation in subadults are growth hormone (somatotrophin), produced by the pituitary gland, and thyroxin, produced by the thyroid. Severe deficiencies of either of these hormones can lead to stunting of growth, a condition known as dwarfism. Vitamin D, which is obtained both from food and by synthesis in the skin from the action of sunlight, is essential in the normal mineralisation of bone. Deficiency of vitamin D during childhood gives rise to rickets, in which the inadequately mineralised bones are deformed under the stresses imposed by the action of the muscles. Rickets became very common in Western industrialised cities in the seventeenth century as a consequence of poor diet combined with lack of sunshine caused by air pollution and overcrowded living conditions.

Vitamin C is plentiful in raw foods, but is destroyed when food is cooked. Deficiencies of the vitamin used to arise in people such as sailors who did not consume fresh fruit or vegetables for long periods of time. Prolonged deficiency of vitamin C leads to scurvy and loss of teeth, and eventually affects the skeleton because the vitamin is essential in the formation of collagen, one of the constituents of bone. Deficiency of vitamin C also weakens the blood vessels, causing internal bleeding: when this occurs next to the bone, irregular layers of reactive bone tissue resembling periostitis are deposited on the surfaces of the bones.

Anaemia is a disease that occurs when the red blood cells, which carry oxygen to the living tissues of the body, are damaged or depleted. The disease can be caused by a hereditary defect in the haemoglobin molecule to which oxygen is attached in the red blood cell, or it can be acquired through a deficiency in iron absorbed from the diet. Iron deficiency can arise if the diet contains insufficient amounts of absorbable iron compounds, or if bleeding from trauma or from intestinal parasites reduces the amount of iron in the blood. The body's response to iron deficiency is to attempt to increase the number of red blood cells, which are produced by red marrow inside the cavities of bones. An increase in the amount of red marrow in bone, particularly in children, can lead to an expansion of the marrow-containing spongy bone between the compact inner and outer layers of the skull vault bones. Perforation of the outer layer of the skull ('porotic hyperostosis') and in the roof of the eye socket ('cribra orbitalia') are visible manifestations of this increase of blood-cell-producing marrow (fig. **19**).

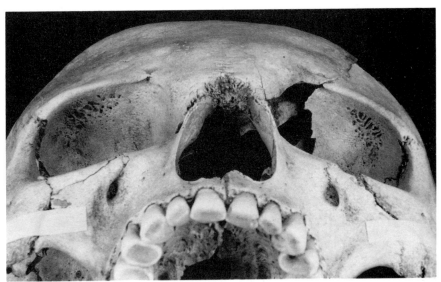

19 A view of the underside of the eye sockets in the skull of a mature adult female. The pitting near the front of the eye sockets is cribra orbitalia, which is caused by expansion of the marrow cavity inside the frontal bone. This condition occurs as a response to anaemia, when a shortage of functioning red blood cells causes the bone marrow to expand in order to increase blood cell production.

Congenital disease and tumours

Several congenital or genetically determined abnormalities can affect the skeleton, although their low incidence (usually less than one per thousand live births) means that they are only rarely encountered in the archaeological record. Achondroplasia is a rare form of dwarfism in which the limb bones are severely shortened while the growth of the skull is relatively normal. Although achondroplasia only occurs in one out of 25,000 live births, a surprisingly large number of cases have been identified in excavated human remains. There is evidence that achondroplastic dwarfs enjoyed wealth and status in some past societies, perhaps accounting for their frequent survival to adulthood and for the respect accorded to them after death.

Spina bifida is a congenital abnormality in which part of the vertebral column, usually in the lower part of the spine, is not fully developed. In severe cases of the defect, the spinal cord protrudes and can become infected or damaged, leading to incontinence and paralysis. Minor, symptomless bony defects in this region that do not expose the spinal cord are called spina bifida occulta, and are quite common in archaeological skeletons (fig. **20**). Cleft palate is a condition in which the two halves of the roof of the mouth fail to fuse together during early development. The deformity, if severe, causes feeding difficulties, and without corrective surgery many infants suffering from cleft palate would have died in the past.

A tumour is the result of uncontrolled proliferation of cells. Benign tumours are slow-growing and localised, while malignant tumours grow rapidly and their cells can spread to other parts of the body through the vascular system, giving

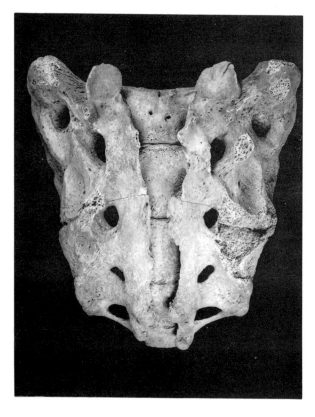

20 Spina bifida in the sacrum of a medieval skeleton from Exeter, Devon. The defect results from a failure of fusion in the midline running the full length of the sacrum. The opening would have been bridged by cartilage or membrane in the living individual and so may not have caused any symptoms.

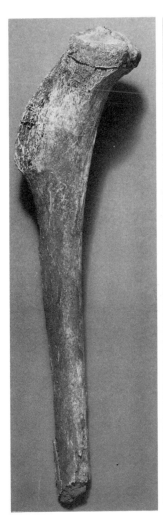

21 Medial (*left*) and posterior (*right*) views of an osteochondroma in the right tibia of a 17-year-old female Neolithic skeleton from Whitwell, Derbyshire. This benign tumour has caused some deformation of the bone but is unlikely to have resulted in much disability for the individual.

rise to secondary or metastatic tumours. Tumours can arise from any tissue, but primary tumours of bone are relatively uncommon. In modern populations the most frequently observed benign tumour of bone is osteochondroma, and about a dozen cases of this condition have been identified in archaeological human skeletons. The tumour usually originates towards the end of a long bone, adjacent to the growth plate, and it consists of an exostosis or bony mass projecting outwards from the surface of the bone. Osteochondromas normally arise during childhood or adolescence, and cease growing at the end of puberty when the epiphyses fuse (fig. **21**).

Malignant tumours of bone are rare, occurring in modern populations with an annual incidence of one per 100,000 individuals. Osteosarcoma and chondrosarcoma account for about half of the malignant primary tumours, and the femur, tibia and humerus are the bones most often affected. These tumours usually develop during adolescence, and without treatment are rapidly fatal. Tumours of the soft tissues such as breast and prostate cancers can give rise to secondary or metastatic growths developing at many locations in the skeleton.

As the metastases grow they cause an initial resorption of spongy and compact bone, followed in some instances by dense deposits of new bone.

Paget's disease of bone, which mainly afflicts elderly people, is a deforming condition in which the rate of bone remodelling is dramatically increased. Rapid resorption is accompanied by irregular new bone formation so that the affected parts of the skeleton become enlarged, softened and liable to breakage. The disease is quite common in modern European populations, being present in about five per cent of individuals aged above fifty years. The disease may have been less common in the past, as relatively few archaeological instances have yet been reported.

Dental palaeopathology

Diseases of the teeth and their surrounding tissues produce changes that are readily recognisable in the skeletal remains of past populations. The same criteria used by modern clinicians in the diagnosis of dental disease in living people can be applied to archaeological remains. This means that the extent and pattern of dental disease in past populations can be linked to aspects of those people's diet and lifestyle, and compared to disease rates in modern industrial, agricultural and hunter–gatherer communities.

Teeth are the hardest parts of the skeleton and are normally resistant to decay, but the fermentation of sugars by bacteria in the mouth can produce acids that attack the enamel and dentine. In dental caries localised demineralisation and cavitation of the tooth occur, eventually leading to the loss of the tooth crown. The prevalence of dental caries has been shown to reflect the amount of soft sticky and sweet foods in the diet, and the disease is relatively uncommon in pre-agricultural communities.

Decay or severe wear of the tooth crown can lead to infection by bacteria of the pulp chamber of the tooth. The infection may form a dental abscess in the jaw, recognised by a smooth rounded enlargement of the tooth socket around the apex of the tooth root. Periodontal disease, or infection and degeneration of the

22 Enamel hypoplasia on the lower front teeth of an adult skeleton from Cirencester, Gloucestershire. The hypoplastic lines are horizontal linear depressions in the surface of the enamel caused by a disturbance to normal enamel growth during childhood. These teeth would have been developing when the individual was aged between two and four years old.

36

tissues that support the teeth, leads to resorption of the margins of the tooth sockets, exposing the roots of the teeth. Both abscesses and periodontal disease can lead to premature loss of the teeth (antemortem tooth loss, or AMTL). Loss of teeth before death can be detected in skeletal remains because the tooth socket is remodelled and smoothed over by new bone after the tooth has been lost.

Dental calculus (tartar) is a mineralised deposit that accumulates on the inner and outer surfaces of the teeth above the gum line. Calculus is white, yellow or light brown in colour and consists of the calcified remnants of bacterial plaque and food debris. It is deposited more rapidly when the diet contains a lot of meat, but individual factors such as poor dental hygiene also determine the extent of calculus accumulation. It is easily removed by accident when cleaning archaeological specimens, so care must be taken not to disturb deposits of calculus when palaeopathological studies are to be undertaken.

Enamel hypoplasia is a localised thinning of the enamel layer of a tooth, resulting from a temporary cessation in the activity of enamel-forming cells during childhood at a time when the teeth are developing inside the jaw. Experimental studies in animals have shown that dietary deficiencies, hormonal imbalance and episodes of diseases including parasitic infestations can all produce defects in the developing enamel. This means that enamel hypoplasia is a non-specific indicator of physiological disturbance during growth. Hypoplasia occurs in less than 10 per cent of individuals from modern industrialised countries, but rates as high as 95 per cent are found in some prehistoric archaeological samples (fig. 22).

Treatment

Although there is little direct evidence for the effective treatment of illness in antiquity, fractures are often well healed and show few signs of infection. This suggests that the treatment of fractures using splints and bandages was commonplace. Amputation of part of the body may have been undertaken as a treatment, but could also result from violence or as a punishment. Healing after amputation through a long bone is recognised by the development of a bony callus at the amputation site followed by closure of the exposed marrow cavity of the bone. Although amputation has only occasionally been detected in human remains, it is sometimes illustrated in ancient art.

One form of treatment for which there is plenty of skeletal evidence is trepanation, the surgical removal of a portion of the skull. This practice was common throughout the world, with many cases reported from South America, the Melanesian Islands and North Africa, as well as being identified in numerous skeletons in Europe from the Neolithic period and later. The operation was performed by removing or retracting part of the scalp and then drilling, cutting or scraping away a piece of the skull bone. This was a skilled procedure with the potential complications of infection or direct injury to the brain, but in more than half of the archaeological examples of trepanation the site of the operation is healed, indicating prolonged survival of the patient. Trepanations were often made at the site of skull fracture, and it is likely that the operation was performed to alleviate symptoms such as headache or epilepsy. Some trepanations that show no sign of healing may have been performed after death for ritual rather than therapeutic reasons.

The treatment of dental conditions is difficult to recognise in archaeological remains before the use of fillings and prostheses became common in medieval times. The deliberate removal of teeth may indicate an attempt to alleviate dental disease but could also be undertaken for ritual or cosmetic reasons. A Neolithic individual from Denmark who suffered from dental abscesses had holes drilled between the roots of the upper molar teeth, presumably to alleviate the symptoms of infection. The earliest known examples of restorative dentistry are from Egypt, where a dental bridge consisting of natural teeth attached with gold wire has been dated to around 2500 BC.

Cutmarks and postmortem modification

Following death a wide range of physical and biological agencies can modify the appearance of bone. Bones that have been exposed above ground may show signs of weathering caused by sunlight, wind, water transport or frost action. Weathered bone shows a network of fine surface cracks and sometimes the surface exfoliates, peeling off in fine layers. The action of sun may cause bleaching on the outside of the bone, and abrasion from wind-borne particles or from water transport will tend to produce pitting and rounding of projecting parts of the bone.

A bone that is broken at or around the time of death (i.e. while still 'green') will show longitudinal or spiral breaks with sharp, straight edges. The broken

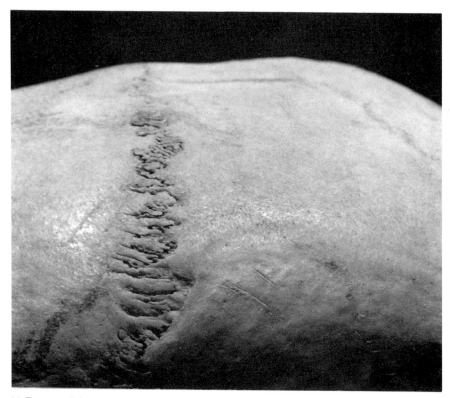

23 Two parallel cutmarks on the left parietal bone of an Iron age male skull from Aulnat, France. The skull, which was discovered as an isolated specimen in a well, showed a series of short straight cutmarks near the sites where the chewing muscles were attached to the sides of the skull vault.

surfaces will usually be of the same colour as the rest of the bone surface. If the bone is broken a long time after burial, for example during excavation, the broken edges will be rougher and more irregular and in most circumstances they will be lighter in colour than the adjacent bone surface.

Abrasion of bone, caused by movement against rocks or hard particles in soil or by the trampling action of large animals, produces fine, shallow, randomly orientated scratches that are concentrated on the most prominent parts of the bone. Large carnivores may modify human remains, causing pitting, scoring and puncturing of the surfaces. Distinctive puncture marks occur on bones with a thin layer of cortex, such as ribs, shoulder blades and hip bones. Carnivores also chew the articular ends of long bones, causing fraying and irregular rounding of the ends of the shafts, and will chew off the spinous processes of the vertebrae. Rodents use their chisel-like incisor teeth to scrape and shave away the surfaces of bones. Their activity can be recognised from the distinctive fan-shaped patterns of regular shallow grooves that are concentrated on projecting areas of a bone, for example around the edges of the eye socket. These grooves often show a constant slope or 'pitch' between the inner and outer surfaces of the bone. Plant roots and lichens secrete acids that can etch the surfaces of bones. Root marks are recognised as a network of shallow, meandering grooves that are often whiter in colour than the surrounding bone. These grooves are U-shaped in cross-section.

Cutmarks on human bones may indicate the deliberate defleshing and dismemberment of human remains. Such marks can be distinguished from natural damage by the location, directionality and microscopic cross-section of the marks (fig. **23**). Sharp metal edges produce narrow, steep-sided and symmetrical V-shaped grooves. Most stone tools (except those made from obsidian) produce broader, irregular or stepped-sided grooves that show multiple fine, closely spaced striations which result from minor irregularities in the cutting edge. Unlike the scoring caused by carnivore teeth, which tend to follow the contours of the bone, cutmarks usually show strong, purposeful direction with separate marks having parallel orientations. Cutmarks from defleshing have been detected on a middle Pleistocene hominid skull from Ethiopia.

— 5 —

Mummies, Bog Bodies and Ice People

The process of mummification

Decay or putrefaction of the soft tissues of the body occurs when the tissues are invaded by micro-organisms such as bacteria and fungi. Putrefaction is assisted by enzymes produced by the bacteria, and the rate at which it occurs is also determined by the temperature and humidity of the burial environment as well as by the state of dehydration of the body. Natural mummification can occur when a body is buried in dry soil (for example, desert sand) or when a body has been exposed to sun or dry air shortly after death. Natural mummification is most common in extremely dry environments such as the cold deserts of the northern high latitudes or the coastal arid zone of Peru. This form of mummification takes months or years to complete, and results in preserved dry tissues that are hard, dark and shrivelled in appearance.

Artificial mummification refers to methods that enhance the preservation of the soft tissues of the body. The word 'mummy' is derived from the Persian mumia, which means bitumen or pitch. Although the black appearance of mummified tissue has been attributed to darkening of preservatives such as resin, recent chemical studies have shown that in ancient Egypt bitumen was in fact used to preserve mummies. Other steps taken by the embalmers to ensure the preservation of mummies include smoke-curing, embalming with oils and other organic preservatives, and the removal of the internal organs which are prone to rapid decay.

The best-known mummies are those of the dynastic periods in Egypt. The embalming process used to produce these mummies is described in contemporary Egyptian texts and in classical Greek literature, and these accounts have been substantiated by scientific studies of the mummies themselves. The embalming process, which took seventy days to complete, began with the removal of the deceased individual's internal organs. The body was then desiccated over a period of several weeks by covering it with dry natron, a naturally occurring carbonate salt. When completely dehydrated the body was coated with liquefied resin or with pitch, moulded to create a resemblance to the surface of a living person. The mummy was then wrapped with layers of linen bandages, some-

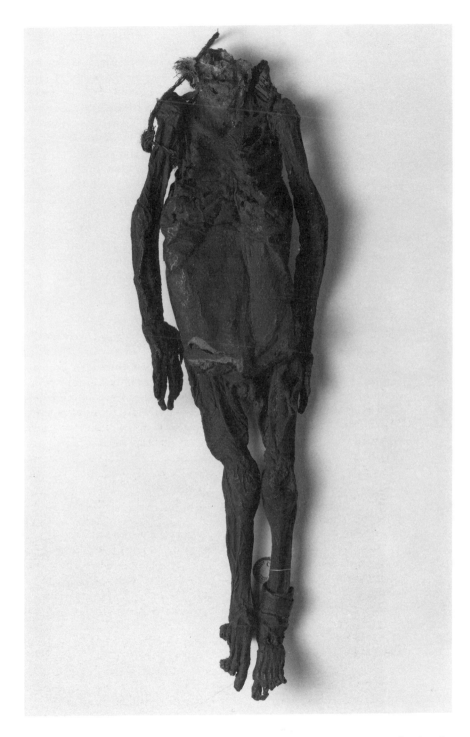

24 Preserved body of a young child from Darnley Island in the Torres Straits, showing the Melanesian technique of mummification. The raised shoulders indicate that the body was suspended in a vertical position during natural drying. The head, which is missing, would have had its facial features restored using ochre and resin.

times with more resin added between the layers, and finally enclosed in a wooden or stone coffin or sarcophagus.

Mummification was also practised in South America, Australia and Melanesia, and in the Aleutian Islands. In the coastal regions of Chile and Peru around 500 BC the early farming communities placed their dead in 'mummy bundles'. The body was seated in a flexed position in a basket or gourd which was then wrapped with layers of cloth. The dry climate assisted the preservation of the soft tissues, and in only a few instances is there evidence for the use of artificial methods of preservation. In aboriginal Australia, preservation of bodies began with exposure of the corpse in a tree or on a platform, the body being dried by the sun, sometimes with the assistance of smoke from a fire. The body was then eviscerated and the skin removed, after which it was covered with a coating of red ochre mixed with grease (fig. **24**). The native people of the Aleutian Islands (off the southern coast of Alaska) prepared mummies by removing the internal organs and then letting the body dry out naturally in air. The body was then clothed and wrapped in a bundle of matting and waterproof skins tied with cords. The mummy bundles were stored in dry caves, suspended above the ground to protect them from the effects of moisture.

Bog bodies

Throughout north-western Europe burials, dating mostly to the Iron Age, Roman and early medieval period, have been found in peat bogs and other waterlogged deposits. The greatest numbers of bog burials occur in Germany and Denmark, and over a hundred bog bodies have been discovered in Great Britain. Many appear to have been the victims of punitive or sacrificial killings,

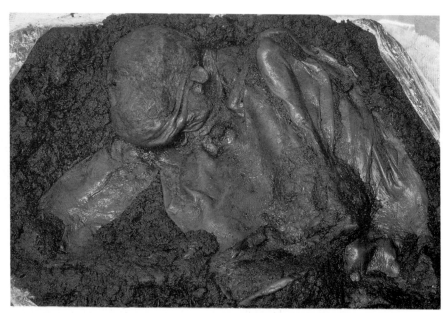

25 Bog body discovered at Lindow Moss, Cheshire, in 1984. The body is of an adult male who had been ritually killed before being deposited in a pool in the bog.

although it is likely that a few were accidental deaths of persons trapped while crossing the bogs and others were inhumation burials of individuals who had died of natural causes. The ritual nature of the mode of death is shown in cases where there is evidence for a combination of strangulation and weapon injuries as well as deliberate immersion (often face down) in a pool in the bog. Bog bodies are often found unclothed and in a crouched or unusual posture (fig. 25).

Peat bogs can arrest the normal decay of the soft tissues of a body through a combination of cold temperature, absence of oxygen (which is essential for many bacteria to grow) and the antibiotic properties of the breakdown products of organic materials, including humic acids, in the bog water. In acid bogs the bones and teeth of the body become decalcified and soft, but the skin, muscles, tendons and hair can be well preserved. Internal organs are also preserved and may contain the remains of the individual's last meal. One of the best-preserved bog bodies is that of Tollund Man, discovered in Denmark in 1950. The body was lying on its right side in peat deposits dating to the Iron Age, around 200 BC. The cause of death was apparently strangulation, and a rope of braided thongs was found pulled tightly round the neck of the body. The preserved stomach and small intestine contained the remains of a meal consumed between twelve and twenty-four hours before death. It consisted of a porridge of barley grain with added vegetable fat; no animal products were present.

Ice people

A natural freeze-drying process can occur when bodies are placed in cold, dry environments and protected from subsequent thawing. Burials dating from the seventh to third centuries BC in southern Siberia have produced exceptionally

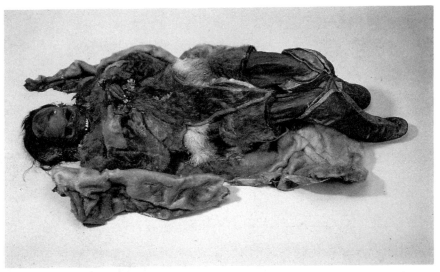

26 A mummy found at Qilakitsoq on the west coast of Greenland, radiocarbon dated to about AD 1475. The body was dressed in an anorak, heavy sealskin trousers and high boots. It had been placed in a rockshelter where a combination of dehydrating cold winds and protection from rain, snow and sunlight resulted in exceptional natural preservation of the soft tissues.

27 The body of the ice man, discovered near Tiesenjoch in the Austrian/Italian Alps in 1991. The body, which has been radiocarbon dated to 3300 BC, was naturally mummified by the cold climate and protected from decay by a covering of accumulated glacier ice.

well-preserved bodies with intact soft tissues. In addition to embalming at the time of death the bodies were also protected by permanently frozen soil or permafrost, which had penetrated into the burial chambers. On the west coast of Greenland, bodies from two medieval graves located under a rock shelter at Qilakitsoq had been naturally dehydrated by the intensely cold and dry environment. The graves contained the bodies of six women and two children, and their skin was sufficiently well preserved to show fine tattoo lines on their faces. Clothing made from mammal and bird skins was also found to be well preserved at this site (fig. **26**).

In September 1991 a body was discovered protruding from glacier ice at an altitude of 3200 metres in the Austrian/Italian Alps. It was originally thought to be less than ten years old, but remains of clothing and tools found alongside the body showed that it was buried in prehistoric times. The body has now been dated by radiocarbon methods to 3300 BC. The individual had died in late summer or autumn, and was partially dehydrated by the cold climate before being covered by snow falls that later turned into glacier ice. Preliminary studies of the body show that it was a young to middle-aged adult man whose standing height was about 159 cm. The skin of the body has marks that have been interpreted as tattoos. Tools found alongside the body include a copper-bladed axe, a yew bow with arrows in a quiver, and remnants of fur clothing (fig. **27**).

Locating Burial Sites

Most burials are discovered either accidentally or through the systematic excavation of cemeteries, monuments or habitation sites. Prehistoric peoples buried their dead in a number of locations, including cemeteries, burial mounds, caves, rock shelters, house floors and middens. Burials were sometimes placed in prominent locations, such as on hill crests or coastal headlands, or on territorial boundaries.

Aerial photography can detect the presence of below-surface variation in soil depth and composition, which shows up at the ground surface in the form of soil marks (on freshly ploughed soils) and cropmarks. Soil marks are produced by the contrast between the ploughing of a deep soil, such as that overlying a buried ditch, and a soil that is shallow in relation to the depth of ploughing. In the areas of shallow soil the plough cuts into the horizon underlying the ploughsoil, exposing it to view when the soil is overturned, thus providing a contrast with the areas of deeper soil. Cropmarks occur on soils that form above permeable deposits such as sands and limestones. In summer, during periods of low rainfall, these soils become desiccated and the crop plants suffer moisture stress. The degree of stress, which is reflected in the growth and appearance of the plants, will vary according to slight differences in soil depth, such as occur above buried archaeological features.

Aerial photography has proved useful in the detection of prehistoric burial mounds and mortuary enclosures, as well as in locating ecclesiastical buildings of the Christian era (see below). The trapezoidal outlines and broad flanking ditches of earthen long barrows and the bank and ditch structure of disc and bell barrows are examples of European prehistoric funerary monuments that can be detected by aerial photography (fig. 28). However, single inhumations are too small and inconspicuous to be identified from cropmarks, except when they occur at the centre of recognisable burial mounds or enclosures.

The conventional geophysical survey methods of magnetometry and resistivity are not very useful for determining the positions of individual burials, particularly on urban sites where the presence of metal objects and secondary disturbance produce complicated signals that are difficult to interpret. Magnetometry has been used successfully at Foxley in Wiltshire to confirm on the ground

28 Aerial view of a prehistoric barrow cemetery at Oakley Down, Dorset. The cemetery originally included more than twenty bowl, bell and disc-barrows containing burials and cremations dating to the Bronze Age. The barrows are located close to funerary monuments constructed earlier in the Neolithic period.

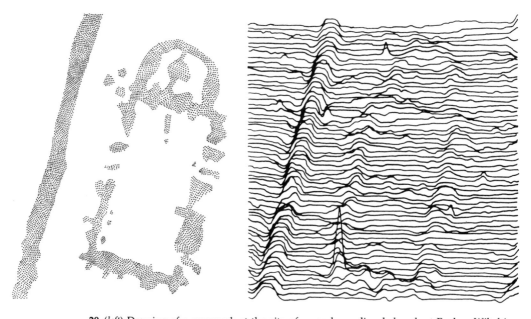

29 (*left*) Drawing of a cropmark at the site of an early medieval church at Foxley, Wiltshire. The traces of the walls of the church, which was 25 metres in overall length, are visible to the south (right) of a linear mark showing the location of a nearby enclosure wall. The irregularities in the outlines of the walls of the building indicate the locations of external post-pits, and a semi-circular apse is visible at the eastern (upper) end of the church. (*right*) Magnetometer survey of the same cropmark feature. The magnetometer signals are displayed as horizontal traces, with the vertical deflection proportional to the strength of the magnetic field. The outline of the walls of the nave and apse of the medieval church are faintly visible, while the stronger signal to the north (left) is from the enclosure wall.

a cropmark feature that had been interpreted as an early medieval church. The cropmark showed a rectangular structure about 20 metres long, aligned east–west with a semi-circular apse at its east end and surrounded by a larger rectangular enclosure (fig. **29**). Magnetometer traverses, made at 0.5-metre intervals, were recorded and displayed on a plot in which the vertical displacement of the trace is proportional to the strength of magnetic anomalies. The survey picked up the outline of the church (also confirmed by the trial trench), but a grave-like feature visible as a small east–west orientated cropmark at the eastern end of the nave of the church was probably too small to produce a magnetic anomaly.

One method that has proved successful in detecting individual burials is ground-penetrating radar. This method, like conventional radar, uses electromagnetic pulses which are reflected back by soil surfaces that differ in water content. In survey work the radar emitter and receiver are traversed across the region of interest and a two-dimensional plot is produced, showing reflection delay time against horizontal distance (fig. **30**). The delay time is proportional to the depth of burial of the reflecting horizon. Burials that have been dug into simply stratified soils can be identified from the pattern of reflections caused by the contrast between the grave fill and the surrounding undisturbed soil. The localised reflecting layers produce a characteristic hyperbolic-shaped pattern on the plot. The method produces its best results on sandy, high-resistivity soils and is generally less effective on clayey soils.

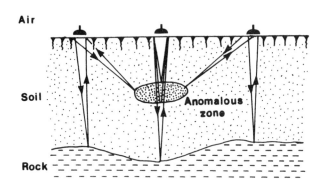

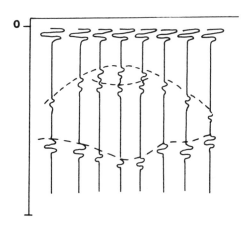

30 The principle of ground-penetrating radar in detecting subsurface features. (*above*) Radar signals are generated by a transmitting antenna and directed into the ground. The antenna is traversed across the region of interest, and three of the many possible antenna positions are shown on the diagram. Reflected radar pulses are received at the antenna from natural boundaries between layers and from intrusive (anomalous) features located within layers. (*below*) When the signals are displayed as two-dimensional plots, showing the delay times of reflected echoes at each horizontal position of the radar antenna, the anomalous zone appears as a hyperbolic-shaped pattern located above the undulating soil/rock boundary. Note that reflections are received from the upper and the lower boundary of the anomalous zone.

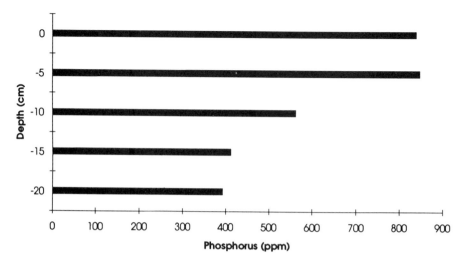

31 Graph showing average phosphorus concentration in soil samples taken at fixed depths below skeletons in a churchyard at Kellington, North Yorkshire. The amount of phosphorus in the soil shows an increase up to 10 cm below the skeleton.

Soil analysis

Phosphates are present as a natural mineral constituent of all soils, at concentrations that range from 100 to 1000 parts per million. In areas of human occupation the phosphate level in the soil can be enhanced considerably beyond natural levels. Phosphates derived from human activity tend to become fixed to other soil compounds close to the point of deposition, and little phosphorus is subsequently lost through uptake by plants or by leaching (except in very acid soils). An additional, recent source of soil phosphates in rural areas stems from the use of modern agricultural fertilisers. These are usually concentrated in the plough-zone, typically the top 25 cm of soil profiles, and do not affect phosphate levels at greater depths.

The bodies of humans and animals are particularly rich in phosphorus which, along with calcium, is a major constituent of the mineral apatite that gives bone its strength and hardness. Phosphorus is also concentrated in other tissues of the human body, and decomposition of human bodies after burial leads to an enrichment of phosphate levels in the vicinity of the inhumation. Even when the body is preserved only as a soil silhouette, the enhancement of phosphate can readily be seen in a vertical soil profile.

At burial grounds in Kellington and Bolsover, Yorkshire, soil phosphorus levels were measured at controlled intervals above and below the legs of buried skeletons. The amount of phosphorus was elevated at up to 10 cm below the burial, but rapidly returned to background level at greater depths (fig. **31**).

Traditional English burial practices

Roman law specified that cemeteries should be located well away from residential areas and places of worship, and the earliest Christian churches of the Roman and Anglo-Saxon period in England were not usually the focus of a burial ground. The Christian tradition in the medieval period, at least from the eighth century AD, was to bury the dead close to the church in an area consecrated as a churchyard. From the tenth century AD the standard amount of enclosed ground was one acre, hence 'God's Acre' as a colloquial expression for a parish churchyard. Some early Christian churches in England were built on existing pagan sacred sites, and a few of these churchyards are surrounded by earlier earthworks suggesting the reuse of Iron Age or earlier enclosures. It appears, therefore, that the transition from pagan ritual site to Christian graveyard was not necessarily a sudden and radical change.

Christian inhumation burials follow an earlier European tradition in which the supine body is conventionally orientated west–east with the legs extended. Orientations of burials are often influenced by prominent local topographical features such as the alignment of buildings, paths and cemetery boundaries, as well as by the orientation of adjacent graves. It has been suggested that variation in grave orientation in some early Christian cemeteries may indicate the season of burial, since the direction of sunrise moves further north as the seasons change from winter to summer. Another interpretation of changes in grave orientation is that successive ecclesiastical buildings were constructed on different axes of alignment, burials being laid out using the walls of the church as a convenient reference direction (fig. **32**).

In parishes where a church was located centrally within its churchyard, the south and east sides of the churchyard were often preferred, while the north side tended to have fewer burials (or, when space became limited, more recent burials). The north side was sometimes used for unbaptised or stillborn children, and for paupers and strangers. Burials inside churches were uncommon before

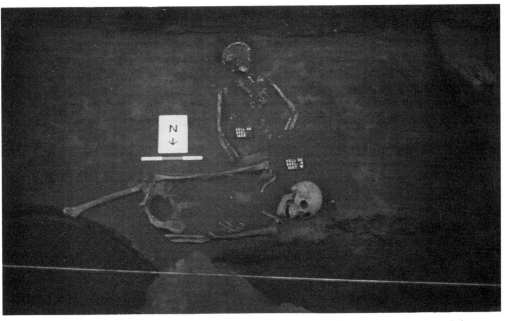

32 Skeletons excavated during building work at Kellington Church in North Yorkshire. The skeleton in the foreground is orientated east–west with the head to the west, in accordance with Christian burial traditions. This burial cuts across the lower half of an earlier, north–south orientated skeleton that may represent a pre-Christian burial dating to the Anglo-Saxon period.

33 Brick-built burial vaults of the seventeenth to nineteenth centuries AD at the Church of St Augustine the Less in Bristol, Avon. Archaeological investigations revealed the outlines of the 107 vaults, filling the interior of the church, which originally held several hundred coffin burials.

the eleventh century, and most intramural burials (within the walls) were of ecclesiastics or privileged lay individuals. Important burials were sometimes placed in side chapels or in tomb chests and wall benches above floor level. Following the later medieval period the popularity of indoor burial increased, and the ground beneath the floor level, particularly of urban churches, often became honeycombed with brick- and stone-lined vaults and shafts, each containing many burials (fig. 33).

With the great increase in population of western European cities from the eighteenth century onwards, the space available in burial grounds of city parish churches proved inadequate for the hygienic disposal of the dead. New cemeteries were established in Ireland and Scotland in the late eighteenth century, but reforms were slower in England where the first private cemetery was opened in Norwich in 1821.

Historical and demographic sources

Epigraphic evidence

Grave markers and memorials are a useful source of historical and demographic information (fig. 34), although comparison of inscriptions on memorials with the details given in the burials register shows that epigraphic data is a selective and

34 (*left*) Grave marker commemorating fifteen members of a single family. The distribution of their ages at death is typical of a population with a relatively high life expectancy. There are relatively few childhood deaths, and most of the family members survived beyond middle age. (*below*) Survivorship curve reconstructed from the ages of death of the family members shown on the grave marker. The curve is similar in shape to that of a population with a life expectancy at birth of about fifty years (see the upper curve in Fig. **11**).

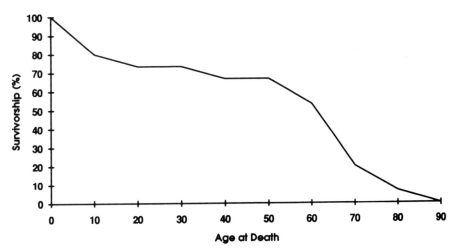

sometimes misleading source of information about a cemetery population. Many more individuals are buried in a cemetery than are recorded on the memorials, particularly in public common graves which can each contain the remains of over a hundred individuals. Furthermore, some of the memorials in a graveyard may commemorate individuals who are buried elsewhere.

Archival evidence

Parish registers of baptisms, marriages and burials were instituted in England in the sixteenth century by Thomas Cromwell, but many registers subsequently became ineffective or lapsed altogether. In the early nineteenth century Parliament enacted new legislation requiring all burials to be registered on specially printed forms, and by 1836 civil registration of all births, marriages and deaths was required by law. During the nineteenth century the overcrowding of many churchyards, together with concerns over public health, led to the provision of private and publicly funded cemeteries in major English towns and cities. Although many of these Victorian cemeteries have since been closed and their land put to other uses, the Registers of Burials that had to be kept by each cemetery are sometimes still available for study in public archives and local libraries.

Registers of burials are rich sources of information for family historians, demographers and those interested in the history of disease and public health. For example, the early parish registers can be used to identify mortality crises precipitated by epidemics or famines, when the number of burials within a small community in one year could greatly exceed the average numbers within the same community in previous and subsequent years. The wealth of demographic information in nineteenth-century records is shown by the first Register of Burials for Sheffield General Cemetery, which covers the years 1836 to 1857 and gives details of burial location, date of death, name, gender, cause of death, occupation, residence at birth and at time of death, and the names and occupations of the parents of the deceased.

— 7 —

Excavating and Preserving Human Remains

Graves are intrusive features, distinguished from surrounding undisturbed deposits by contrasts in stratification as well as soil colour and texture. Most graves are cut and backfilled within a short space of time, but it is not uncommon for primary burials to be disturbed either accidentally (by subsequent grave digging) or deliberately in order to remove or add further items to the grave.

The state of preservation of buried human bone depends on the length of time it has been in the ground and on the acidity of the soil. In acidic environments such as peat bogs the inorganic component of bone (hydroxyapatite) is dissolved away, leaving behind the bone collagen which shrinks and deforms the original outline of the bone. In free-draining acidic soils the collagen is also destroyed, leaving hardly a trace of the original bones. In alkaline soils the bone collagen reacts with ground water and eventually decays, while the bone mineral is preserved although in a more fragile state than in the original bone. The best environments for preserving bones are dry soils with plenty of calcium carbonate.

After the outline of a grave has been defined and recorded, excavation can proceed slowly by removal of the grave fill. As bones are encountered they should be left in place and their surfaces brushed clean of soil. When exposure of the skeletal remains is completed they should be photographed on both monochrome and colour film and described with the aid of sketch plans and measurements of burial depth and orientation. The clarity of a photograph of a skeleton in situ is considerably enhanced if the bones are first wiped clean with a moist brush or sponge. An oblique photograph can be corrected for distortion if small markers are placed alongside the skeleton: the co-ordinates of the markers are measured and recorded, and when the photograph is enlarged the image is superimposed on a scale plan showing the position of the markers (fig. 35).

Handling, sampling and storing specimens

Bones are less likely to suffer damage if they are dry before being lifted. When bones are removed from a grave they are placed with identification labels in strong paper or cloth bags, and these bags are then placed in rigid cardboard

35 Excavation of a Saxo–Norman coffin burial at Barton upon Humber, Humberside.

containers for transport and storage. Permeable materials for bags and boxes allow the bones to continue to dry out. For fragmented skeletons separate bags are used for the bones of the skull, the chest and abdomen, the arms and the legs. Care must be taken when lifting the skull, particularly if the braincase is full of soil. After all the visible bones have been lifted it is essential that the underlying few centimetres of soil are sieved in order to recover any fragments and small bones and teeth that may have been moved out of their original position. It is also quite common for infant burials to be inserted into adult graves, and a careful search must be made for these small and often delicate bones.

Cremations require special care because the fragments of bone and teeth may be quite fragile, especially if they have been subjected to prolonged firing at a high temperature. When the cremated remains are enclosed in a burial vessel it is advisable if possible for the complete vessel with its contents to be taken to the laboratory for controlled excavation of the cremation.

It is not generally advisable for preservatives or hardeners to be applied to bones at the time of excavation. Bones that are broken during excavation can be repaired in the laboratory, and the use of preservatives can make cleaning, chemical analysis and dating more difficult. When it is essential that a very fragile or eroded skeleton be hardened in situ, an acetone-soluble material such as PVA or Paraloid is sparingly applied.

Sampling
Samples of bone and soil are taken during excavation for chemical and organic analysis and dating. For bone, carbon is extracted from the organic component by chemical methods. Samples of several hundred grams of bone are needed for conventional radiocarbon dating, however, as little as 0.5 g of compact bone may be sufficient for an accelerator mass spectrometry (AMS) date. Compact cortical bone from the femur or tibia provides suitable material for radiocarbon dating. The sample is usually a partial cross-section of the shaft of the bone, leaving

enough of the shaft intact so that the maximum length of the bone can still be measured. Samples for serological and biochemical analysis of blood proteins and DNA can be obtained from spongy bone such as the centre of a vertebral body. Soil samples taken from below the abdominal region can provide organic residues from the digestive system, and samples of soil taken at measured distances below the base of the body can provide information on the migration of chemical elements between the bone and the surrounding soil.

Samples of bone destined for DNA analysis by polymerase chain reaction (PCR) must be handled with some care, as even trace amounts of modern human DNA can cause problems of contamination. The samples are first excavated and handled using protective gloves, and are never washed. Clean airtight containers are used to transport and store the samples prior to analysis, and they are stored in a cool dark place such as a refrigerator.

Cleaning, conservation and reconstruction
Bone from sandy soil is brushed clean of adhering soil, while clayey soil is removed in the laboratory using water and small brushes. Bone is washed in warm water above a 4-mm mesh screen that will trap any bone fragments or teeth

36 Reconstruction of a skull. (*left*) Fragments of the skull after cleaning but before reconstruction. (*right*) The fragments have here been fitted together along their broken edges and temporarily secured in place using strips of paper tape. A thin strip of wood has been used to reinforce the lower border of the right eye socket. When all the available pieces of bone have been correctly replaced, a more permanent reconstruction can be undertaken using water-soluble glue to join the bone fragments.

that might otherwise be lost. Bones are allowed to drain and are then dried slowly at room temperature on a drying rack or absorbent material. Bones intended for sampling for chemical or biomolecular analysis are not washed at this time, but are packaged separately to avoid contamination. Clean dry bone is clearly labelled, usually with a code for the site and a number indicating the grave or context of the inhumation, using permanent ink, and if the bone is friable the writing can be protected with a clear lacquer.

A knowledge of skeletal anatomy is a prerequisite for reconstructing fragmentary remains. Broken edges must first be dry and any adhering soil removed. Broken bones can be restored either temporarily with adhesive paper tape or more permanently with an acetone-soluble or water-soluble clear adhesive. Glue is not applied to bones that may need to be sampled for radiometric dating or chemical or biomolecular analysis. The skull is best reconstructed by rejoining the cranial vault bones first, then completing the cranial base and finally the face. If the lower jaw is present this is used as a guide to attaching the face in the correct position on the cranial vault. Sandboxes are used for supporting bones that have been glued together, allowing long bones and ribs to be supported with their shafts vertical while the glue hardens. Gaps where the bone is missing are strengthened by gluing in wooden, glass or plastic supporting rods (fig. **36**).

Recording skeletons

When a large series of articulated skeletons is studied it is essential to record the information about each skeleton on data sheets, with a separate record being made for each individual skeleton. These data sheets, together with plans, drawings, photographs and X-ray films constitute the primary source from which data can be abstracted when completing a report on the skeletal remains. For skeletons scheduled to be reburied it is especially important that the data sheets are comprehensive and include the primary information rather than interpreted data (for example, the data sheets list the features present that can be used for sex determination, rather than simply a classification of the skeleton as female, male or unknown sex). The data collected for each skeleton will include an inventory of all skeletal and dental elements present, a list of measurements and skeletal variants, the skeletal indicators used for determining biological sex and age at death, the details of any abnormalities indicating the presence of disease, and a record of any samples taken for chemical or biomolecular analysis. The skeletal inventory can be presented as a table listing the parts of the skeleton that are present, or it can be drawn as an outline diagram of a complete skeleton with the bones that are present coloured in.

If the skeletal remains consist of large numbers of commingled (mixed), disarticulated or fragmentary bones a different recording procedure is used. Commingled remains are often found in middens, ossuaries or in grave fills where primary burials have been disturbed by later burials or by grave robbing. In this situation it may be necessary to calculate the minimum or probable number of individuals that were originally present. The commingled remains are classified according to skeletal part, whether they are from the left or right side of the skeleton and whether they are adult or belong to one of the subadult age categories. A minimum number of individuals is then estimated for each age category by identifying the skeletal part that occurs most frequently (for large assemblages of bones this may require the use of a computer program).

— 8 —

Ethics and the Law

The statutory law controlling human burials varies from country to country, and even within Britain some aspects are far from clear. But it is universal for people to treat their dead with respect and in most instances to recognise the passing of life with rituals that reflect their religious beliefs. In virtually all countries the disturbance of burials is prohibited either by custom or by law, although many Western industrialised nations have adopted procedures that enable disused burial grounds to be cleared for redevelopment.

Legislation

In England and Wales the principal civil statutes governing the excavation of human remains are the Burial Act 1857, the Town and Country Planning (Churches, Places of Religious Worship and Burial Grounds) Regulations 1950 and the Town and Country Planning Act 1990. Section 25 of the Burial Act 1857 requires that a licence from the Home Office be obtained before excavation of human remains 'from any place of burial', except when a body is removed from one consecrated place of burial and immediately reinterred in another consecrated burial ground. All removals of human remains from consecrated ground are, however, also subject to ecclesiastical law which requires that permission (known as a 'faculty') be granted by the diocesan authorities.

Section 82(6) of the Town and Country Planning Act 1962 and sections 238, 239 and 240 of the Town and Country Planning Act 1990 supersede the provisions of the Burial Act 1857 in cases where burial grounds are acquired for redevelopment by central or local government authorities or by 'statutory undertakers' (contractors working on transport schemes or for public utilities). These sections of the Town and Country Planning Acts allow human remains to be disinterred from burial grounds acquired for redevelopment without any requirement for a diocesan faculty or a Home Office licence, provided that the Town and Country Planning (Churches, Places of Religious Worship and Burial Grounds) Regulations of 1950 are observed. These regulations include notifying in advance the diocesan authorities and the general public and, when burials have occurred within twenty-five years, the next of kin or other personal representatives of the deceased. The regulations also require that all excavated human remains be reinterred in an appropriate place of burial. The Town and Country Planning Act 1990 defines a burial ground as 'any churchyard, cemetery or other ground whether consecrated or not, which has at any time been set apart for the purposes of interment', and therefore applies equally to prehistoric funerary monuments in which human remains have been interred. In Scotland, section 118 of the Town and Country Planning (Scotland) Act 1972 provides similar legislation to that contained in the 1990 Act for England and Wales.

Specialists in the analysis of human skeletal remains may on occasion wish to make use of bone from recently deceased individuals in their research. The use of recently deceased bodies for medical education and research is regulated by the Human Tissue Act 1961 and the Anatomy Act 1984. Authorisation for such use must be given by the person lawfully in possession of the body, and if the deceased themselves had not wished such use then enquiries must be made to determine whether relatives or others close to the deceased object to such use.

The ethics of studying human remains

Ethics can be defined as a coherent system of values that determine a code of conduct. Ethical principles are specific to a given culture, and different cultures are very likely to profess different ethics concerning important issues such as the treatment of the dead. Ethical debate can also emerge within a culture, when different segments of the society hold different values, or when change, inconsistency or incoherence exist within a generally held system of values.

Archaeologists, biological anthropologists and specialists in medical anthropology, medical history and palaeopathology all have an interest in the long-term curation of human remains. The study of burial sites and funerary practices can offer important insights into the structure of past societies. Cultural modifications of the human skeleton such as cranial deformation, tooth mutilation and treatment of injuries and infections are of interest in both social anthropology and medical history. Biological anthropologists and palaeopathologists make extensive use of curated collections in their research into palaeodemography, biological affinities among populations, origins and epidemiology of disease and the effects of diet and occupational stress. New techniques in molecular biology, including DNA sequence analysis and sensitive, highly specific assays of human proteins, are now providing the means to genetically characterise small samples of human bone from archaeological excavations. Finally, scientific interest does not necessarily increase with the antiquity of the human remains. Skeletons of identifiable individuals of known age and sex are of great value to forensic anthropologists and this information also provides a means of calibrating methods for ageing and sexing archaeological specimens.

In the United States and Canada a proliferation of state and federal legislation now virtually prohibits the scientific excavation of Native American burial sites, and enforces the reburial of curated human remains and associated artefacts that date to the historic period (i.e. when present-day tribes can substantiate claims of relatedness to the deceased individuals). Activists for reburial are seeking to extend the scope of this legislation with the intention of bringing about the reburial of all aboriginal human remains and associated artefacts, including prehistoric material. Medical and anthropological organisations have debated the need for scientific curation of human skeletal remains, and the Palaeo-

37 An ossuary in Central Mexico. These ossuaries, sometimes known as charnel houses, were built to house bones disturbed by later grave-digging in crowded churchyards.

pathological Association has set up a database committee in the USA with the task of defining minimum categories of data to be collected during the analysis of human remains that are scheduled for reburial.

Short-term curation of human remains for scientific analysis followed by reburial is often an unsatisfactory procedure. The period of scientific study prior to the reburial of the remains may be severely limited, and the list of potentially important data is long. Reburial raises a further ethical problem for the scientist: a long-held tradition in Western science is that of the replication of results, which includes the provision of access to original observations and specimens for scientists who wish to challenge their colleagues' findings. This is particularly important in the field of palaeopathology, where a mere description or photographic image of a specimen is often insufficient to decide between alternative diagnoses. Specimens of inestimable scientific value, such as the earliest known case of tuberculosis in the New World, are currently scheduled for reburial, and the fossil remains of the earliest hominids to reach the continent of Australia have already been returned to the ground.

It would of course be a mistake to discuss the curation of human remains solely in terms of scientific interest. Museums also use human remains and mortuary artefacts in their interpretive exhibits. One of the most popular exhibits in recent years at the British Museum in London was that of Lindow Man, the 'bog body' in which extraordinary preservation of the skin and other soft tissues led to a more than usually life-like display. While many museums have the facilities for producing authentic replicas of human remains, the substitution of realistic casts for the originals would often involve considerable expense, and might also reduce public interest in the exhibit.

Although the scientific case for the curation of human remains is a strong one, it must be balanced against the powerful political and emotive arguments presented by indigenous groups and others who can substantiate their genuine interest in the remains. Human remains curated in national museums are held in the interests of the public of the curating nation, and requests for repatriation of human remains are more appropriately directed through the indigenous people's national representatives and organisations, rather than through individual or tribal representation. Decisions should also take into account the curating institution's mission: where this does not require the preservation and interpretation of human remains and other objects held sacred by indigenous peoples, the institution should not collect or retain the material. This does not necessarily require repatriation, however, for human remains could in some cases be transferred to a more appropriate institution in the host country.

In summary, a wealth of information can be obtained from human remains, including details of demography, occupation, diet and disease, and new scientific techniques capable of extracting further important data are continually being developed. These are strong arguments in favour of the analysis and curation of human remains from archaeological sites. But the extent to which present-day communities identify with and respect the cultural traditions of their distant ancestors varies in different regions of the world, and it is therefore necessary to take into account the legitimate interests of indigenous peoples in planning the excavation and analysis of human remains.

Further Reading

Aiello, L. and Dean, C. *Human Evolutionary Anatomy*. Academic Press, London, 1990.

Bass, W.M. *Human Osteology*. Special Publication of the Missouri Archaeological Society, Columbia, 1987.

Boddington, A., Garland, A.N. and Janaway, R.C. (eds). *Death, Decay and Reconstruction: Approaches to Archaeology and Forensic Science*. Manchester University Press, Manchester, 1987.

Brothwell, D.R. *Digging up Bones*, 3rd edn. British Museum (Natural History) and Oxford University Press, London and Oxford, 1981.

—*The Bog Man and the Archaeology of People*. British Museum Publications, London, 1986.

Bush, H. and Zvelebil, M. *Health in Past Societies*. British Archaeological Reports International Series 567. B.A.R., Oxford, 1991.

Chapman, R., Kinnes, I. and Randsborg, K. *The Archaeology of Death*. Cambridge University Press, Cambridge, 1981.

Hillson, S. *Teeth*. Cambridge University Press, Cambridge, 1986.

Iscan, M.Y. and Kennedy, K.A.R. (eds). *Reconstruction of Life from the Skeleton*. Liss, New York, 1989.

Kelley, M.A. and Larsen, C.S. (eds). *Advances in Dental Anthropology*. Wiley-Liss, New York, 1991.

Layton, R. (ed.). *Conflict in the Archaeology of Living Traditions*. Unwin, London, 1989.

Manchester, K. *The Archaeology of Disease*. Bradford University, Bradford, 1983.

Metcalf, P. and Huntington, R. *Celebrations of Death: The Anthropology of Mortuary Ritual*, 2nd edn. Cambridge University Press, Cambridge, 1991.

Ortner, D.J. and Putschar, W.G.J. *Identification of Pathological Conditions in Human Skeletal Remains*. Smithsonian Institution, Washington, DC, 1981.

Rodwell, W. *Church Archaeology*. English Heritage and Batsford, London, 1989.

Saunders, S.R. and Katzenberg, M.A. (eds). *The Skeletal Biology of Past Peoples*. Wiley-Liss, New York, 1992.

Stead, I.M., Bourke, J.B. and Brothwell, D. (eds). *Lindow Man: The Body in the Bog*. British Museum Publications, London, 1986.

Steele, D.G. and Bramblett, C.A. *The Anatomy and Biology of the Human Skeleton*. Texas A & M Press, College Station, 1988.

Ubelaker, D.H. *Human Skeletal Remains: Excavation, Analysis, Interpretation*, 2nd edn. Taraxacum, Washington, DC, 1989.

Van Beek, G.C. *Dental Morphology: An Illustrated Guide*, 2nd edn. Wright, Bristol, 1983.

White, T.D. and Folkens, P.A. *Human Osteology*. Academic Press, London, 1991.

Index of Figure References

Index

Page numbers in bold refer to illustrations